선교
영어
회화

English For Mission

한 귀 란

서울대학교(B.M.), 미국 McMurry College, Southern California Baptist College & Seminary(M.A., Ph. D.)를 졸업하고 남아공의 University of the Free State의 Post Doctorate 과정에서 한아(韓亞) 공동 수탁 프로젝트를 연구하였으며, 미국 Yale University 객원연구원, Houston Graduate School of Theology 객원교수, 한국기독교 어문학회 부회장 및 이사, 전국대학 여자교수대표 포럼(NWPF) 정회원 등을 역임하였고, 현재 칼빈대학교에서 교수로 재직 중이다.

저서 및 역서로는 『Hebraism과 Hellenism 비교연구』, 『Rene Descartes의 Cogito Ergo Sum의 자아의식 연구』, 『번역의 과정에서 일어나는 철학의 어의 변용: Being and Non-Being의 번역을 중심으로』, 『S.Evans, 실존주의 철학 평가』, 『Modern Theological English』, 『언어와 정신분석』, 『좀 더 천천히 말씀해 주시겠어요?』, 『동서언어철학의 비교』, 『성경실용영어』, 『종교 근본주의 무엇이 문제인가』, 『서양철학과 자유주의 신학』 등이 있다.

선교영어회화

English For Mission

한귀란 지음

글로벌콘텐츠

Preface

영어를 학습함에 있어서 그 흥미를 상실하게 되는 이유 중 한 가지는 보통 주어진 본문들의 내용이 지극히 일반적이고 상식적이기 때문이다. 그런 의미에서 전공학술 영어원서들을 다룰 수 있기 전에 학생들의 전공과 직결된 교양영어의 과정이 필수적이다.

필자는 신학대학에서 오랫동안 영어를 담당해 온 사람으로서 우선 영어성경[NIV]학습의 병행을 목적으로 하여 교재를 만들어 보았다. 영어성경은 구어체(Colloquialism) 실용영어 학습의 보고(寶庫)이다. 뿐만 아니라, 영문학이나 영어의 발달사에 있어서 성경을 제쳐 놓고는 감히 그 주옥같은 표현들의 문학성이나 기법을 논할 수조차 없게 된다.

본서는 고급 수준의 영어 교재가 아니다. 따라서 관련 영문법을 기초적인 수준에서 설명하였고 독해문장들과 더불어 문법을 이용한 회화 기술을 터득하도록 배려하였다. 이미 필자는 『성경실용영어(Matthew & English)』라는 책을 저술하였고 학생들의 전공과 영어 두 분야를 함께 훈련시키는 수업을 진행하고 있다. 본서는 그보다 좀 더 쉬운 과정이라고 하겠다.

더불어 진정한 언어소통이란 문자적 훈련만을 통해서 얻어지는 것이 아님을 명심하여야 한다. 그것은 사람과 사람 사이의 실존적인 부딪힘을 통하여 이루어지는 것이며, 그러한 인격적인 만남(Personal Encounter)을 통하여 어휘에 대한 감각을 더할 수 있는 것이다.

아무쪼록 본서를 통하여 영어의 훈련은 물론이요, 신학을 공부하는 모든 자들, 그리고 영어를 학습하는 모든 자들에게 다소나마 도움이 되기를 소망한다.

본서의 출판을 있게 하여 주신 (주)글로벌콘텐츠출판그룹의 홍정표 사장님, 그리고 고락을 함께해 온 동료 교수들, 말없이 배려를 아끼지 않은 가족에게 감사를 드린다.

2014년 2월

칼빈대학교 연구실에서

저자 한 귀 란

Contents

CHAPTER I

기초 5형식 문장 이용 말하기

Lesson 1 Moses and Aaron were among his priests.

〈S + V〉, 〈S + be V +장소부사구〉 문장 이용

A 성경 독해 NIV Reading

Ecclesiastes 1:1-9

1 The words of the Teacher,son of David, king in Jerusalem:

2 "Meaningless! Meaningless!" says the Teacher. "Utterly meaningless! Everything is meaningless."

3 What does man gain from all his labor at which he toils under the sun?

4 Generations come and generations go, but the earth remains forever.

5 The sun rises and the sun sets, and hurries back to where it rises.

6 The wind blows to the south and turns to the north; round and round it goes, ever returning on its course.

7 All streams flow into the sea, yet the sea is never full. To the place the streams come from, there they return again.

8 All things are wearisome, more than one can say. The eye never
has enough of seeing, nor the ear its fill of hearing.
9 What has been will be again, what has been done will be done
again; there is nothing new under the sun.

한글성경 참조

전도서 1:1-9

1 다윗의 아들 예루살렘 왕 전도자의 말씀이라

2 전도자가 가로되 헛되고 헛되며 헛되고 헛되니 모든 것이 헛되도다

3 사람이 해 아래서 수고하는 모든 수고가 자기에게 무엇이 유익한고

4 한 세대는 가고 한 세대는 오되 땅은 영원히 있도다

5 해는 떴다가 지며 그 떴던 곳으로 빨리 돌아가고

6 바람은 남으로 불다가 북으로 돌이키며 이리 돌며 저리 돌아 불던 곳으로 돌아가고

7 모든 강물은 다 바다로 흐르되 바다를 채우지 못하며 어느 곳으로 흐르든지 그리로 연
하여 흐르느니라

8 만물의 피곤함을 사람이 말로 다 할 수 없나니 눈은 보아도 족함이 없고 귀는 들어도
차지 아니하는도다

9 이미 있던 것이 후에 다시 있겠고 이미 한 일을 후에 다시 할찌라 해 아래는 새 것이
없나니

B 관련문법 Related Grammar Review

위 본문은 거의 다 S+be V+장소부사구의 문형을 사용한 문장들로 이는 제1형식 문장 패턴에 속한다. 그런데 이때의 be동사, 즉 am, are, is/was, were의 원형은 그 자체가 존재적 의미를 가지고 있다. 즉, 존재적 의미일 때는 "~있다, 존재한다"로 해석되어 1형식 동사가 되고 상태적 의미일 때는 "(어떤 상태, 성질에) 머물러 있다, ~이다"로 해석되어 2형식 동사가 된다. 이때 be동사가 "~있다"로 쓰이면 반드시 그 뒤에 장소부사(구)를 수반하는 데 비해, "존재한다"로 쓰이면 그 뒤에 아무것도 수반되지 않는 특성을 가지고 있으므로 구문상 두 가지로 분리시킬 수 있다.

예) ·Your sister is in the garden. (네 누이는 정원에 있다.)

S + be V + 장소부사구 (네 누이는 정원에 있다.)

·God is. (신은 존재한다.)

S +V

·I think, therefore I am

S +V S+V (나는 생각한다, 고로 존재한다.)

또한 S + be V + 장소부사(구)의 도치구문인 There(Here) + be V + 명사 + (수식어, 구, 절)도 많이 쓰이는 문형이다. 즉, 「S(명사) + be(~있다) + there(here)」에서 자동사 뒤에 있는 부사 there(here)를 문두로 보내어 도치시키고자 할 경우에는 주어와 동사의 어순을 바꾸어야 한다. 그래서 「There(Here) + be + S(명사) + ~」의 형태를 취하게 된 것이다. 그러므로 "be 동사"의 수(단·복수)는 그 뒤에 있는 명사의 수와 일치시키는 것이다.

사람·사물의 존재 유무를 나타낼 때 쓰는 be 동사의 여러 가지 형태

	a, an	
There + be +	some, no	불특정 주어 + (시간, 장소)
	many, an	
	much	← the, this, that(X)
	수사 등등…	

·There are many apples on the table.
← (도치) Many apples are there on the table.
(탁자 위에 많은 사과들이 있습니다.)

·There is a beautiful river in that village.
← (도치)A beautiful river is there in that village.
(그 마을 안에는 아름다운 강이 있습니다.)

·How many students are there in the auditorium?
← 도치구문이 아니고 대답문장이 도치(그 강당 안에는 얼마나 많은 학생들이 있습니까?) 됨: There are ______________________.

C 제1문형 익히기 Basic Sentence Drill

The Kim's Family (그림 보고 이야기하기)

The Kim's family is at home today.

(1) Mr. Kim is <u>in the kitchen</u>.

(2) Young Mi is ______________.

(3) Sue and Tom are ______________.

(4) Miss Kim is on her ______________ reading.

(5) The dog ______________.

(6) The cat ______________.

(7) And the car is ______________ the ______________.

C 응용영작 Advanced Composition (S+be+V+장소부사구)

•Level 1

① 얼룩말은 동물원에 있습니다.

: A zebra is in the zoo.

② *검사들은 *보통, *검찰청에 있습니다.

:

③ 나는 *어렸을 적에 할머니 집에 있었습니다.

:

•Level 2

① *많은 종류의 꽃들이 정원에 있습니다.

:

② *심각한 환자들은 *중환자실에 있습니다.

:

③ 많은 다른 종류의 인종이 *뉴욕시 전체에 있습니다.

:

•Level 3

① 대한민국 정치는 *혼란한 상태에 있습니다.

:

② 장미꽃들은 *언덕 이편에 있지만, 백합꽃들은 *언덕 저편에 있습니다.

:

③ 하나님의 *진노가 그 *부패된 백성 위에 있게 될 것입니다.

:

▸ Word Tips for composition

·검사: prosecutor

·보통: normally, usually

·검찰청: a public prosecutor's office

·어렸을 적에: When I was young

·많은 종류의: many kinds of

·심각한: serious, critical

·중환자실: an intensive care unit(I.C.U.)

·뉴욕시 전체에: all over the city of New York

·혼란한 상태에: in(the state of) chaos

·언덕 이편에: on this side of hill

·언덕 저편에: on that side(the other side of)hill

·진노: the wrath

·부패된: corrupted

D 응용 독해문 Applied Passages

Page From A Diary

There are five people at our table, including myself.

I've already learned a lot about them in the short time we've been at sea, although we rarely meet except at mealtimes.

First of all, there's Dr. Stone-my favorite, I must confess.

He is a man of about sixty-five, with gray hair and a pleasant face.

He gave up his medical practice a short time ago and is traveling around the world before he retires to Florida.

As a young man, he served overseas for a number of years as a doctor in the Navy.

He speaks several languages and has told us a lot about the port cities we're going to visit.

He seems to have been everywhere.

During the day, when he's not talking to other passengers (you get the impression he already knows everybody on board!), he sits on desk reading or looking out at sea through an old telescope.

Then there's "grandma." I call her that because her name escapes me.

In spite of being a grandmother, she looks remarkably young, not more than forty-five.

She's on her way to visit a daughter who moved to Australia several years ago.

Naturally, she's very excited at the thought of seeing her daughter again, and of seeing her three grandchildren for the first time.

She can talk of nothing else.

This trip is quite an adventure for her since she has never been overseas before.

Then there's a man I don't like very much, a construction engineer by the name of Barlow.

He's been on leave in California and is now on his way back to the job he has in Singapore.

He's very athletic and spends most of his time swimming or playing tennis.

I've never in my life met a man with such a loud laugh.

He has the cabin next to mine and I can hear him laugh even through the thick cabin walls!

The other person who sits at our table is Mrs. Lang.

I haven't found out very much about her yet.

She's quiet and doesn't talk very much, except to consult with the doctor about her children's various ailments.

She's on her way to join her husband in Bangkok.

Making Useful Location Adverb Phrase

여러 가지 유익한 장소부사구의 활용

·around the corner from ~의 모퉁이를 돌아서

·across the street 길 건너편에

·along the street 길가를 따라서

·behind my back 내 등 뒤에

·behind the tree 나무 뒤에

·down the river 강가를 따라 내려가

·in ten miles 10마일 내에

·about two blocks away 약 2블록 떨어져서

·under the roof 지붕 밑에

·under the sea 바다 밑에

·(upon)on the wall 벽 위에

·above the sea level 해발

·above the rainbow 무지개 넘어서

·on the desk 책상 위에

·over my head(shoulder) 내 머리(어깨) 위에

·over the fence 담장 너머

·between you and I 너와 나 사이에, 또는 비밀을 얘기할 때

·beneath the pillow 베개 밑에

* under는 어떤 표면의 접착이 되지 않은 상태. ~아래에, 밑에
  beneath는 어떤 표면의 접착 상태의 밑에
  down은 하단, 밑부분을 독립적으로 이야기할 때(up의 상대 개념)
  below는 막연한 거리 밑에

또는,

·at church 교회에서

·at school 학교에서

·at home 집에서

* church, school, home 등 많이 쓰는 이 명사들은 건물 개념보다는 추상성명사 개념이 있으므로 in보다는 at을 쓴다.

·up(upon) the mountain 산 위에

·under the table 탁자 밑에 / 또는 비밀 금전 거래를 이야기할 때

·in front of ~의 정면에, ~앞에

·by the well 샘물가에

·beside me 내 옆에

·among the flower 꽃들 사이에서

·between the two gentlemen 두 신사 사이에

·through(throughout) the city 도시를 관통하여

·toward the North 북쪽을 향하여

·from Seoul 서울에서부터

·into the room 방 안으로

·out of the room ~방 밖으로 etc.

이상은 가장 흔하게 쓰이는 장소부사구이며 이때의 전치사들은 부사로 전용되어 사용된다.

E 1형식 관련 성경구절 Related Expression in the Bible

① Judges 1:19(사사기 1:19)

The Lord was with the men of Judah.

(여호와께서 유다와 함께 하신 고로)

② Judges 1:36(사사기 1:36)

The boundary of the Amorites was from Scorpion pass to Sela of beyond.

(아모리 사람의 지계는 스코르피온 지경부터 셀라 그 위였더라)

* NIV → 구체적 지역의 이름을 사용 번역됨.

(즉, 아르랍빔 비칼의 바위부터 그 위였더라)

③ John 12:2(요한복음 12:2)

Here a dinner was given in Jesus honor. Martha served, while Lazarus was among those reclining at the table with him.

(거기서 예수를 위하여 잔치할새 마르다는 일을 보고 나사로는 예수와 함께 앉은 자 중에 있더라.)

* reclining at the table: 식탁에 앉다, 기대다

* recliner: 기대어 편하게 다리를 뻗을 수 있는 의자

④ Luke 7:6(누가복음 7:6)

So Jesus went with them. He was not far from the house when the centurion sent friends to say to him.

(예수께서 함께 가실새 그 집이 멀지 아니하여 백부장이 벗들을 보내어 가로되)

* far from 장소明: ~로부터 멀다

* centurion: 백부장

⑤ John 5:17(요한복음 5:17)

Jesus said to them, "My father is always at his work to this very day, and I, too, am working.

(예수께서 저희에게 이르시되, 내 아버지께서 이제까지 일하시니 나도 일한다 하시매)

* be at work: 근무 중인, 일하는

*** 〈S + be V + 장소부사(구)의 도치구문〉⇒ 1형식의 도치구문.

즉, There(Here) + be V +명사+ (수식어, 구, 절) 문형

① Psalm 58:11(시편 58:11)

Surely the righteous still are rewarded; surely there is a God who judges the earth.

(진실로 의인에게 갚음이 있고 진실로 땅에서 판단하시는 하나님이 계시다)

* the righteous 의인(the + 형용사 = 단·복수명사)

② Ecclesiastes 1:1(전도서 1:1)

A time for everything: there is a time for everything, and a season for every activity under heaven.

(천하에 범사가 기한이 있고 모든 목적이 이룰 때가 있나니)

③ John 5:32(요한복음 5:32)

There is another who testifies in my favor, and I know that his testimony about me is valid.

(나를 위하여 증거하시는 이가 따로 있으니 나를 위해 증거하시는 그 증거가 참인 줄 아노라)

* anther who 이하: who 이하 수식구가 another(person), 즉 다른 이를 설명함.

* testimony: 간증, 증거

* valid: true, be valid 정당성이 있는, 참인

Lesson 2

Its gutter is a cubit deep and a cubit wide... And this is the height of the altar.

〈S + V + C〉 문장 이용

A 성경 독해 NIV Reading

Ezekiel 43:13-16

13 "These are the measurements of the altar in long cubits, that
cubit being a cubit and a handbreadth: Its gutter is a cubit deep
and a cubit wide, with a rim of one span around the edge. And
this is the height of the altar:

14 From the gutter on the ground up to the lower ledge it is two
cubits high and a cubit wide, and from the smaller ledge up to
the larger ledge it is four cubits high and a cubit wide.

15 The altar hearth is four cubits high, and four horns project
upward from the hearth.

16 The altar hearth is square, twelve cubits long and twelve cubits
wide.

한글성경 참조

에스겔 43:13-16

13 제단의 크기는 이러하니라 한 자는 팔꿈치에서부터 손가락에 이르고 한 손바닥 넓이
가 더한 것이라 제단 밑받침의 높이는 한 척이요 그 사방 가장자리의 너비는 한 척이
며 그 가로 둘린 턱의 너비는 한 뼘이니 이는 제단 밑받침이요
14 이 땅에 닿은 밑받침 면에서 아래층의 높이는 두 척이요 그 가장자리의 너비는 한 척
이며 이 아래층 면에서 이 층의 높이는 네 척이요 그 가장자리의 너비는 한 척이며
15 그 번제단 위층의 높이는 네 척이며 그 번제하는 바닥에서 솟은 뿔이 넷이며
16 그 번제하는 바닥의 길이는 열두 척이요 너비도 열두 척이니 네모 반듯하고

B 관련문법 〈Related Grammar Review〉

S (주어) + V (불완전자동사) + C (주격보어)

소개문장을 쓸 때에는 "나는 누구이다", "나는 무엇이다" 또는 "나의 주소는 ~이다", "나는 ~출신이다" 등등 주어의 신분에 대한 내용을 나타내어 주는 주격보어가 꼭 수반되기 때문에 영어의 기본 5문형 중 제2형식에 해당되는 윗 도식이 사용된다. 이 경우 주격보어(C)에는 명사, 형용사, 현재분사 또는 과거분사가 올 수 있는데 본문에서는 명사보어가 주로 사용되었고, 그 외의 2형식 문장의 문장 패턴을 살펴보면 다음과 같다.

기본형

(1) S + be(become) - group + 명사

·He is a Christian.

(그는 기독교인이다.)

(2) S + be(become) - group + 형용사

·He turned pale at the news.

(그는 그 소식에 얼굴이 창백하게 변했다.)

(3) S + vi + to + root ~

·She appears to be happy. 〈부정사의 형용사적 용법 - 서술용법〉

(그녀는 행복한 듯 보인다.)

·She is to travel in Europe next year. 〈be to 용법〉

(그녀는 다음 해에 유럽을 여행할 예정이다.〉

·My hobby is to collect stamps. 〈부정사의 명사적 용법〉

(나의 취미는 우표를 수집하는 것이다.〉

(4) S + vi(be) + ~ing 형태

·My hobby is collecting stamps. 〈동명사〉 - 2형식문

(나의 취미는 우표를 수집하는 것이다.)

(5) S + be + that(wh -) 명사절

·The trouble is that we are short of money.

(곤란한 점은 우리에게 돈이 부족하다는 것이다.)

(6) It + be + 주격보어 + that(wh-) + S'+ V'+ ~

·It is wrong that you tell a lie.

(네가 거짓말하는 것은 잘못이다.)

(7) It + be + 주격보어 + to + root ~ 〈부정사의 명사적 용법〉

·It is wrong(for you) to tell a lie.

(네가 거짓말한 것은 잘못이다.)

(8) It + be + 주격보어 + rooting 〈동명사〉

·It is wrong(your) telling a lie.

(네가 거짓말한 것은 잘못이다.)

▣ **주어와 주격보어의 관계:** 주어의 성질(상태), 동작을 보충 설명해 주는 것이 주격보어이기 때문에 그 둘은 서로 밀접한 관계를 가지고 있다. 즉, 다음과 같은 관계로 설명된다.

	①명사(주어와 동격관계를 나타냄)
주어 + 불완전자동사 +	②형용사(주어의 성질·상태를 설명)
	③현재분사(주어의 능동적인 동작을 나타냄)
	④과거분사(주어의 수종적인 동작을 나타냄)

① 명사가 다 주격보어인 경우: 주어와 보어가 동격관계

·She is a students. 〈She와 student는 동격관계〉

(그녀는 학생이다.)

② 형용사가 주격보어인 경우(주어의 상태)

·She looks happy this morning.

〈She의 현재의 상태가 아주 happy한 상태임을 말하고자 한다〉

(그녀는 오늘 아침 행복해 보인다.)

③ 현재분사가 주격보어인 경우(주어의 능동적인 동작)

·He sat reading the novel.

〈그가 소설을 읽으며 앉아 있음을 나타내는 주어의 능동적 동작〉

(그는 소설을 읽으며 앉아 있었다.)

④ 과거분사가 주격보어인 경우(주어의 수동적인 관계)

·He sat surrounded by his children.

〈그가 자신의 손자들에 의해 둘러싸여 있는 수동적 관계〉

(그는 손자들에 의해 둘러싸여 앉아 있었다.)

▣ 불완전자동사: 그 자체 동사만으로는 문장 주어의 성질과 상태를 완전히 설명할 수 없기 때문에 반드시 그 뒤에 주격보어로 명사, 대명사, 형용사 및 명사, 형용사 상당어구들을 취해야만 완벽한 문장을 이룰 수 있는 동사이다. 이러한 성질을 가지고 있는 동사들을 일반적으로 be-group과 become-group으로 나눈다.

▣ 동사의 유형들

be – group	become – group	유사보어를 취하는 동사
(어떤 성질·상태)~에 머물러 있다, ~이다, ~하다 〈무변화〉 유지(계속) – keep, continue, remian, stand, lie, hold, be … 지각 – sound, smell, taste, feel … 인상 – seem, look, appear, ring …	(어떤 성질·상태의 변화를 나타내어) ~이 되다, ~된다 〈변화〉 become, grow, get, turn, make, go, come, fall, run, wear, prove, turn out, come out …	동사는 완전자동사인데 뒤에 보어의 성질로 형용사 또는 명사가 사용된 경우 come back, die, marry, be born, fall down, end up, dance, sit, come, go …

C 제 2문형 익히기 Basic Sentence Drill

Would you please introduce each one of your friends?

a. Mr. Kim
a teacher
Seoul

b. Ok Choo Yoo
a nurse
Kwang Ju

c. Brown
a secretary
at S.S.Company
the United States

d. Miss Lee
a radio
producer
Japan

e. Mr. Park
a pastor
Pusan

f. Mr. Choh
a journalist
Bei-Jing

a. About Mr. Kim:

1. ____________________

2. ____________________

3. ____________________

4. ____________________

5. ____________________

etc.

b. About Ok Choo Yoo:

1. ____________________

2. ____________________

3. ____________________

4. ____________________

5. ____________________

etc.

c. About Ms. Brown:

1. ____________________

2. ____________________

3. ____________________

4. ____________________

5. ____________________

etc.

d. About Miss Lee:

1. ____________________

2. ____________________

3. ____________________

4. ____________________

5. ____________________

e. About Mr. Park:

1. ____________________

2. ____________________

3. ____________________

4. ____________________

5. ____________________

f. About Mr. Choh:

1. ____________________

2. ____________________

3. ____________________

4. ....

5. ....

D 응용 영작 Advanced Composition

•Level 1

① 우리 누이는 간호사입니다. c ⇒ noun의 경우

:

② 그 환자도 *사실상 의사였습니다.

:

③ 그 여행은 *상당한 모험이었습니다.

:

•Level 2

① 우리 엄마는 그 소식에 얼굴이 *창백해졌습니다. c ⇒ adjective의 경우

:

② 내 취미는 우표를 수집하는 것입니다. c ⇒ to부정사 or 동명사 경우

:

③ 그는 *약 55세 가량된 남자였습니다. c ⇒ 형용사구 경우

:

•Level 3

① 우리 목사님 설교의 핵심은 '서로 사랑하라' 입니다. c ⇒ that절의 경우

:

② 문제는 남한이 어떻게 북한을 위해 *경제협력을 하는가입니다.

c ⇒ that(wh/how)절인 경우

:

▸ **Word Tips for composition**

* 사실상: in fact / as a matter of fact / actually / to tell you the truth
* 상당한 모험: quite an adventure
* 창백해지다: turned pale / became pale
* 약 55세 가량 된: of about fifty five
* 설교: message / sermon / preaching
* 경제협력: economic aid

E 응용 독해문 Applied Passages

The substance of this faith is quite the same as the faith under the New Covenant.

Under the Old Covenant, there was a faithful waiting for the coming of the Messiah, and under the New Covenant we look back to the Messiah who has come.

The Old, as well as the New, Testament make us believe in Christ of the whole history.

The subject of that faith is the triune God, and His promises. In Hebrews 11:1, is written: Now faith is being sure of what we hope for and the evidence of things we do not see."

This is the way that Abel, Noah, Abraham, Issac and Jacob lived. It's the way of Moses and the prophets, who went before us.

It's the way of Paul and the Reformers. The question is whether in our times there still is true faith? Jesus said in Luke 9:41, "O faithless and perverse Generation."

F 2형식 관련 성경 표현 More Related Expressions in the Bible

① Psalm 18:2(시편 18:2)

The Lord is my rock, my *fortress and my *deliverer, my God is my rock in whom I *take my refuge.

(여호와는 나의 반석이시요, 나의 요새시요, 나를 건지시는 자시요, 나의 피할 바위이시다.)

* fortress: 요새

* deliverer: 구출자, 건지시는 자

* take refuge: 피난하다, 피하다

② Psalm 34:10(시편 34:10)

The lions may grow weak and hungry, but those who seek the Lord lack no good thing.

(젊은 사자는 궁핍하여 주릴지라도 여호와를 찾는 자는 모든 좋은 것에 부족함이 없으리로다)

③ Revelation 8:11(요한계시록 8:11)

The name of the start is *wormwood. *A third of waters *turned bitter, and many people died from the waters that had become bitter.

(이 별 이름은 쑥이라. 물들의 삼분의 일이 쑥이 되매 그 물들이 쓰게 됨을 인하여 많은 사람이 죽더라.)

* wormwood: 쑥

* A third of waters: 물들의 삼분의 일

* turned bitter: 쓰게 되다

④ Jeremiah 47:1-2(예레미야 47:1-2)

This is the word of the Lord that came to *Jeremiah the prophet *concerning the Philistines before Pharaoh attacked Gaza.

(바로가 가사를 치기 전에 블레셋 사람에 대하여 선지자 예레미야에게 임한 여호와의 말씀이라.)

* Jeremiah the prophet: 선지자 예레미야

* concerning: ~에 대하여

This is what the Lord says:

⑤ I Corinthians 13:4-5(고린도전서 13:4-5)

Love is patient, love is kind - It is not proud

It is not rude, it is not *self - seeking, it *is not easily angered.

(사랑은 오래 참고, 사랑은 온유하며, - 교만하지 아니하며,

무례히 행치 아니하며, 자기의 유익을 구치 아니하며, 성내지 아니하며,)

* self - seeking: 이기적인, 자기의 유익을 구하는

* be angered: 성내다, 화나다

Common Usage of the Pattern

→ In making introduction or interview

(소개할 때와 인터뷰할 때):

즉, 자신이나 남의 신분을 알릴 때 주로 2형식 문형의 답이 쓰인다.

① Name / Full Name

(Given Name, Middle Name, Family Name)

② Address / Apartment, Street, City, Country

③ Phone Number / Area Code

and Number

Country Code

④ I. D. Card / Social Security(Residential)

Registration, Driver's License

⑤ Nationality, Native Town, Originated Place

⑥ Marital Status

⑦ Occupation

⑧ Relatives or Friends etc.

Lesson3

So they gathered them and filled twelve baskets with the pieces of the five barley loves.

〈S + V + O〉 문장 이용

A 성경 독해 NIV Reading

John 6:11-14

11 Jesus then took the loaves, gave thanks, and distributed to those who were seated as much as they wanted. He did the same with the fish.

12 When they had all had enough to eat, he said to his disciples, "Gather the pieces that are left over. Let nothing be wasted."

13 So they gathered them and filled twelve baskets with the pieces of the five barley loaves left over by those who had eaten.

14 After the people saw the miraculous sign that Jesus did, they began to say, "Surely this is the Prophet who is to come into the world."

한글성경 참조

요한 6:11-14

11 예수께서 떡을 가져 축사하신 후에 앉아 있는 자들에게 나눠 주시고 물고기도 그렇
게 그들의 원대로 주시니라

12 그들이 배부른 후에 예수께서 제자들에게 이르시되 남은 조각을 거두고 버리는 것
이 없게 하라 하시므로

13 이에 거두니 보리떡 다섯 개로 먹고 남은 조각이 열두 바구니에 찼더라

14 그 사람들이 예수께서 행하신 이 표적을 보고 말하되 이는 참으로 세상에 오실 그
선지자라 하더라

B 관련문법 Related Grammar Review

S(주어) + V(완전타동사) + O(직접목적어)인 제3형식 문장을 활용하여 ~는 ~을 한다고 얘기한다.

기본형

(1) S + vt + 명사(대명사)

·I love flowers.(나는 꽃을 좋아한다.)

·She loved me.(그녀는 나를 사랑했다.)

(2) S + vt + 부정사. 동명사

·I finished to read a book.(나는 책읽기를 끝냈다.)

·I enjoyed reading a book.(나는 책읽기를 좋아한다.)

(3) S + vt + 의문사 + to부정사

·I don't know how to go there.(= I don't know how I should go there.)

(나는 그 곳에 어떻게 가는지 모른다.)

(4) S + vt + that(wh-)명사절

·They believe that she is honest.(그들은 그녀가 정직하다고 믿고 있다.)

·I couldn't understand what she said.

(나는 그녀가 말하는 것을 이해할 수 없었다.)

(5) S + vt + 재귀목적어

·He killed himself.(그는 자살했다.)

(6) S + vt + 동족목적어

She laughed a ugly laugh.(그녀는 추한 미소를 지었다.)

(7) S + vt + 상호목적어, 환유목적어

·They love each other.

(상호목적어)

(그들은 서로 사랑한다.)

·She wiped off the table.

(환유목적어)
(그녀는 탁자를 닦았다.)
* 목적어에 여러 가지 형태가 올 수 있다는 점에 유의하자.

이 외에도 타동사를 대신해서 쓸 수 있는 숙어적인 타동사구가 쓰여질 수 있으므로 이러한 구절을 동사숙어로 암기하는 것이 편리하다. 자주 쓰이는 몇 가지 숙어적인 타동사구는 뒷 페이지에 열거하여 보았으니 활용하자.

뒤 ※ 표시를 보자.⇒(p. 48).

C 제 3문형 익히기 Basic Sentence Drill

►► Questions

1. What do you do everyday in your free time?

2. Besides your free time plan please talk about your daily schedule each other in your class.

↑

(very) early in the 05:00 A.M. ______________________ morning

In the morning	06:00	I get up(get out of bed) at six o'clock.
	07:00	______________________
	08:00	______________________
	09:00	______________________
	10:00	______________________
	11:00	______________________
at noon	12:00 P.M.	______________________
In the afternoon	01:00	______________________
	02:00	______________________
	03:00	______________________
	04:00	______________________
	05:00	______________________
In the evening	06:00	______________________
	07:00	______________________
	08:00	______________________
at night	09:00	______________________
	10:00	______________________
In the middle	11:00	______________________
of the night	12:00 A.M.	______________________

* 일상적이고 습관적인 매일 반복되는 행위를 이야기 할 때는 주로 (~는 ~을 한다), 즉 S + V + O의 3형식 문형이 쓰이고 이때의 타동사는 관용적으로 쓰이는 특정 타동사 표현만 쓰인다. 예를 들면, '세수하다'에서는 wash 동사, 즉 wash one's face를 쓰고 '양치질하다'에서는 brush 동사만, 즉 brush one's teeth라고 표현한다. 그 외의 관용적인 표현은 다음과 같으니 잘 익혀서 활용하도록 하자.

* get out of bed: 기상하다
* take a shower(bath): 샤워(목욕)하다
* get dressed: 옷입다
* watch morning news: 아침 뉴스를 보다
* have a breakfast(snack, dinner, lunch etc.): ~먹다
* go to work(leave for work): 출근하다
* drink a cup of coffee: 커피 한잔하다
* wash the dishes: 설거지하다
* take a (coffee or tea) break: 쉬다(~를 마시면서)
* do homework: 숙제하다
* do laundry: 세탁하다
* listen to the radio: 라디오 듣다
* go to bed: 취침하다

D 응용 영작 Advanced Composition

Level 1

① 교사는 학교에서 학생들을 가르칩니다.

:

② 가수는 극장에서 노래를 합니다.

:

③ *요리사는 주방에서 *자신의 전문 요리를 합니다.

:

Level 2

① 그들은 나를 *비웃었다.

:

② 그 *악당들은 은행에서 돈을 *털었다.

:

③ 그녀는 가난을 *모면했다.

:

Level 3

① 당신은 *실수하는 어린이들을 비웃으면 안 됩니다.

:

② 우리는 고아를 돌보아야만 합니다.

:

③ *북한의 관리들은 남한관리들이 이야기하는 것을 신중하게 듣습니다 (- that절 이용).

:

▶ **Word Tips for composition**

* 요리사: cook
* 자신의 전문요리: his own specialties
* 비웃다: laugh at
* 악당: gangster, knave
* 털다(돈, 금품 따위를): rub~(the bank), steal
* bank rubbery 은행 강도
* 모면하다: escaped, avoid of
* 실수하다: make mistake
* 북한의 관리들: government officials of North Korea

E 응용 독해문 Applied Passages

The Bible proclaims that God made the earth as a proclamation to his glory (Col. 1:17, Rev. 4:11, Ps. 19:8, Job 28:41).

Thus, this world was created in harmony.

Van Til states that the creation in many ways is a reflection of the Creator.

Therefore, Calvinists look at the world as something much broader than a mere depraved world.

Calvinists claim that "We are in the world, but not of the world."

We are depraved sinners and we are fallen creatures.

Yet, we are also the bride of Christ and citizens of heaven.

We have dual-citizenship.

By nature of our being, we are citizens of the world.

And by the grace of our Redeemer, we have the hope to be citizens of a new heaven and earth.

F 3형식 관련 성경 표현 Related Expression in the Bible

① Acts 2:17(사도행전 2:17)

In the last days, God says, I will pour out my spirit on all people. Your sons and daughters will *prophesy, your young men will see visions, your old men will dream dreams.

(하나님이 가라사대 말세에 내가 내 영으로 모든 육체에 부어 주리니 너희의 자녀들은 예언할 것이요 너희의 젊은이들은 환상을 보고 너희의 늙은이들은 꿈을 꾸리라.)

* prophesy: 예언하다

② John 2:17(요한복음 2:17)

His disciples remembered that it is written:

"Zeal for your house will consume me."

(제자들이 성경말씀에 주의 전을 사모하는 열심히 나를 삼키리라 한 것을 기억하더라.)

* zeal: 열심.　　* consume: 소모하다, 삼키다

③ John 2:19(요한복음 2:19)

"Destroy this temple, and I will raise it again in three days."
(이 성전을 헐라, 내가 사흘 동안에 일으키리라.)

④ Psalms 32:5(시편 32:5)

Then I *acknowledged my sin to you and did not cover up my iniquity. I said, "I will confess my *transgressions to the Lord."
(내가 이르기를 내 허물을 여호와께 자복하리라 하고 주께 내 죄를 아뢰고 내 죄악을 숨기지 아니하였더니)

* acknowledged: 인정하다, 자복하다
* iniquity: 죄악, 부정, 부도덕
* transgressions: 죄(guilt, sin)

⑤ Ezekiel 1:4(에스겔 1:4)

I looked and I saw a windstorm coming out of the north.
(내가 보니 북방에서부터 오는 폭풍을 보았는데)

※ 3형식 문장을 만들 때 타동사 대신에 쓸 수 있는 여러 가지 숙어적인 타동사구가 있다. 이들은 우리가 보통 동사숙어로 외우는 말들이고 뒤에 목적어를 수반한다. 흔하게 쓰이는 이들 숙어적인 타동사구를 외우고 영작하여 발표해 보자.

* laugh at: 비웃다
* put up with: 참다, 견디다
* take care of: ~을 돌보다
* be obedient to: ~을 순종하다
* look for: ~을 찾다
* wait on: 시중들다
* get down to: 착수하다
* make fun of: 놀리다, 조롱하다
* be envious of: ~을 부러워하다
* do away with: ~을 없애다. 처분하다 etc.

Lesson 4

But I tell you who hear me;
Love your enemies.

〈S + V + I.O + D.O〉 문장 이용

A 성경 독해 NIV Reading

Ezekiel 44:4-5

4 Then the man brought me by way of the north gate to the front
of the temple. I looked and saw the glory of the LORD filling
the temple of the LORD, and I fell facedown.

5 The LORD said to me, "Son of man, look carefully, listen
closely and give attention to everything I tell you concerning
all the regulations regarding the temple of the LORD. Give
attention to the entrance of the temple and all the exits of the
sanctuary.

한글성경 참조

에스겔 44:4-5

4 그가 또 나를 데리고 북문을 통하여 성전 앞에 이르시기로 내가 보니 여호와의 영광
이 여호와의 성전에 가득한지라 내가 얼굴을 땅에 대고 엎드리니

5 여호와께서 내게 이르시되 인자야 너는 전심으로 주목하여 내가 네게 말하는 바 여호
와의 성전의 모든 규례와 모든 율례를 귀로 듣고 또 성전의 입구와 성소의 출구를 전
심으로 주목하고

B 관련 문법 Realted Grammar Review

S(주어)+ V*(수여동사)+ I.O(직접목적어) + D.O(직접목적어)의 제4형식 문장의 사용(SP. 4)

기본형

(1) S + vt + <u>(대)명사</u> + <u>명사 및 그 상당어구</u>

(I.O) (D.O)

·He gave me some books.

(그는 내게 몇 권의 책을 주었다.)

(2) S + vt + (대)명사 + that(wh-)명사절

(I.O) (D.O)

·I told you that I would come today.

(나는 당신에게 내가 오늘 오겠다고 말했다.)

·I cautiously asked him what he was doing.

(나는 그에게 무엇을 하고 있는지 조심스럽게 물었다.)

(3) S + vt + (대)명사 + t의문사 + to부정사

(I.O) (D.O)

·I cautiously asked him what to do next.

(나는 그에게 다음에 무엇을 할건지 조심스럽게 물었다.)

*** 수여동사**: 이 문형에 속하는 동사는 「(누구)에게」라는 간접목적어와 「(무엇)을」이라는 직접목적어 두 개의 목적어를 필요로 하는 동사이다. 3형식의 동사처럼 이 동사도 완전타동사의 일종으로 수여적인 의미(~해 준다는 의미)가 있기 때문에 "수여동사"(Dative Verb)라고 불리운다.(간접목적어(I.O)≠직접목적어(D.O)) *많이 쓰이는 수여동사에는 다음과 같은 것들이 있다. 주로 (~에게 ~을 해 주다)의 뜻을 이룬다.

① give, lend, hand, tell, teach, offer, owe, send, show, bring, read, sell, write, pass, pay, allow 등과,

② sing, play, spare, order, call, get, find, choose, buy, cook 등인데 이러한 동사들은 주로 전치사 for와 함께 사용한다.→ 3형식 S + V + O로 전환할 때.

예) ·She bought me a flower.

→ (She bought a flower for me.)

·He played me my favorite number in Hymn book.

→ (He played my favorite number in Hymn book for me.)

③ desire, ask, demand, beg, inquire, require, recommend 등 '요구하다'류의 동사들로 3형식 전환 시 of와 함께 사용가능하다.

예) ·He asked me a question.

→ (He asked a question of me.)

·American people demanded the government the freedom publishment.

→ (American people demanded the freedom of publishment fo the government.)

·The company informed us the new innovation project for next year.

→ (The company informed the new innovation project for next year of us.)

[주의] 그러나 간접목적어를 전치사와 함께 뒤로 옮기지 못하는 수여동사들이 있는데, 이는 그 동사들이 두 개의 직접목적어를 받은 것이기 때문이다.

pardon(용서하다), forgive(용서하다), envy(부러워하다), save(덜어주다), charge(요구하다), cause(야기시키다), cost((비용이 들다), answer(대답하다), strike(때리다), wish, own, owe…

·I envy you your success.

(너의 성공이 부럽다.)

·I envy your success to you.(×)

·I envy your success.

(너의 성공이 부럽다.)

·Machines save us much time and trouble.

(기계는 우리에게 많은 시간과 문제를 덜어준다.)

·He saved some milk for lunch.

(그는 점심을 위해 우유를 조금 남겨 두었다.)

C 제 4문형 익히기 Basic Sentence Drill

Please Complete the Sentence(다음 문장을 완성하시오)

* 수여동사와 목적격 인칭대명사 등,

① The doctor gave ________ some medicine to be taken three times ________ day.

(의사는 하루에 세 번 복용할 수 있도록 나에게 약을 주었다.)

② Please ________ me some theological books you have. I will ________ them to you in a few days.

(네가 가지고 있는 신학서적들 좀 빌려줘. 내가 며칠 있다가 돌려줄게.)

③ A few days ago, my aunt ________ ________ a photo which was taken at the beach.

(며칠 전 우리 이모는 해변가에서 찍었던 사진을 내게 보내주셨다.)

④ Could you please ________ ________ the shortest way to the police station?

(경찰서 가는 지름길을 가르쳐 주시겠습니까?)

⑤ Should I give ________ what you ordered for lunch?

(점심 때 주문했던 것을 갖다 드릴까요?)

⑥ Will you ________ ________ whether I should refuse his proposal?
(내가 그의 제안을 거절해야 할지를 충고해 주시렵니까?)

D 응용 영작 Advanced Composition

•Level 1

① 그녀는 뉴욕에서 내게 편지를 썼다.

:

② 내 *부탁 좀 들어주시겠어요?.

:

③ 김군은 *약혼녀에게 *장미꽃 한다발을 보내주었다.

:

•Level 2

① 아침 식사에 계란 두 개를 요리해 주십시오.

:

② 아버지는 내게 *그러한 장소에 가서는 안 된다고 말씀해 주셨다.

:

③ 의사는 내게 *위암 초기라고 알려주었다.

:

•Level 3

① 미국은 일본에게 *평화조약을 지키라고 *경고하였다.

:

② 인간의 문명은 우리들에게 생활의 편리함을 가져다주었다.

:

③ 북한의 지도자 김정일은 그 국민들에게 *언론의 자유를 허용해 본 적이 결코 없었다.

:

▸ Word Tips for composition

* 부탁: favor → 부탁을 들어주다 do 人 a favor
* 약혼녀: fiance
* 장미꽃 한다발: a cluster of roses
* 그러한 장소: such a place
* 위암초기: the early stage of stomach cancer
* 평화조약: a peace agreement
* 경고하다: warn
* 언론의 자유: the freedom of press

E 응용 독해문 Applied Passages

"God sent those dreams", Joseph said, "to tell Pharaoh that a long time of famine is coming, and to show what must be done to prepare so that the people will not starve."

The plans Joseph suggested were so wise that Pharaoh said, "Since your God has told you all these things, none other will be so well fitted to carry out these plans."

And he made Joseph governor of the country and keeper of all the granaries.

F 4형식 관련 영어 성경 표현 Related Expression in the Bible

① Acts 1:24(사도행전 1:24)

Then they prayed, "Lord you know everyone's heart. Show us which of these two you have chosen.

(저희가 기도하여 가로되 뭇사람의 마음을 아시는 주여 이 두 사람 중에 누가 주의 택하신 바 되어)

② Colossians 2:4(골로새서 2:4)

I tell you this so that no one may *deceive you by *the sounding arguments.

(내가 이것을 말함은 아무도 공교한 말로 너희를 속이지 못하게 하려 함이니)

* deceive: 속이다, 기만하다
* sounding argument: 공교한 말, ~언쟁, ~변론

③ II Corinthians 8:24(고린도후서 8:24)

Therefore show these men the proof of your love and the reason for our pride in you, *so that the churches can see it.

(그러므로 너희는 여러 교회 앞에서 너희의 사랑과 너희를 대한 우리 자랑의 증거를 저희에게 보이라.)

* so that ~can(may) ~가 할 수 있도록

④ Ezekiel 33:13(에스겔 33:13)

If I tell the righteous man that he will surely live.

(가령 내가 의인에게 말하기를 너는 살리라 하였다 하자.)

⑤ Daniel 5:17(다니엘 5:17)

Then Daniel answered the king, You may keep your gifts for yourself and give your rewards to someone else. Nevertheless, I will read the writing for the king and tell him what it means.

→ 4형식이 3형식으로 전환 가능한 예문

(다니엘이 왕에게 대답하여 가로되 왕의 예물은 왕이 스스로 취하시며 왕의 상급은 다른 사람에게 주옵소서. 그럴지라도 내가 왕을 위하여 이 글을 읽으며 그 해석을 아시게 하리이다.)

기타 알아두면 좋은 점

※ 거의 모든 4형식 문장은 순서를 바꾸어서 3형식 문장으로 전환시킬 수 있다.

3형식: 주어 + 완전타동사 + 직접목적어

4형식: 주어 + 완전타동사 + 간접목적어 + 직접목적어

3형식: 주어 + 완전타동사 + 직접목적어 + (전치사 + 간접목적어)

(3형식 전환) (부사구)

이때 전치사로 이용될 수 있는 것은 ① to, ② for, ③ of, ④ on 등이 있는데 수여동사에 따라서 다르게 적용된다.

예) ① to / The teacher showed us his newly published book.(sp. 4)

S V I.O D.O

→ The teacher showed his newly published book to us.(sp. 3)

S V D.O

② for / My husband bough me a new dress.(sp. 4)

S V I·O D.O

→ My husband bough a new dress for me.(sp. 3)

S V D.O

③ of / May I ask you some question?(sp. 4)

(V) S V I.O D.O

→ May I ask some question of you?(sp. 3)

S V D.O

④ on / My friend played me a silly trick.(sp. 4)

S V I.O D.O

→ My friend played a silly trick on me.(sp. 3)

S V D.O

Lesson 5

Assyrians have made it a place for desert creatures;

〈S + V + O + O.C〉 문장 이용

A 성경 독해 NIV Reading

Isaiah 23:11-13

11 The LORD has stretched out his hand over the sea and made its
kingdoms tremble. He has given an order concerning Phoenicia
that her fortresses be destroyed.

12 He said, "No more of your reveling, O Virgin Daughter of
Sidon, now crushed! "Up, cross over to Cyprus ; even there
you will find no rest."

13 Look at the land of the Babylonians, this people that is now
of no account! The Assyrians have made it a place for desert
creatures; they raised up their siege towers, they stripped its
fortresses bare and turned it into a ruin.

한글성경 참조

이사야 23:11-13

11 여호와께서 바다 위에 그의 손을 펴사 열방을 흔드시며 여호와께서 가나안에 대하
여 령을 내려 그 견고한 성들을 무너뜨리게 하시고
12 이르시되 너 학대 받은 처녀 딸 시돈아 네게 다시는 희락이 없으리니 일어나 깃딤으
로 건너가라 거기에서도 네가 평안을 얻지 못하리라 하셨느니라
13 갈대아 사람의 땅을 보라 그 백성이 없어졌나니 곧 앗수르 사람이 그곳을 들짐승이
사는 곳이 되게 하였으되 그들이 망대를 세우고 궁전을 헐어 황무하게 하였느니라

B 관련문법 Related Grammar Review

S(주어)+ V(불완전타동사)+ O(목적어)+ O.C(목적보어)

기본형

(1) S + vt + O + O.C(명사·형용사)

·We appointed him chairman.
(우리는 그를 의장으로 임명했다.)

·This portrait makes him too old.
(이 초상화에서 그는 너무 나이가 들어 보인다.)

(2) S + vt + O + O.C(wh - 명사절)

·Prof. Lee has made me what I am today.

(이 교수님은 나를 오늘날의 나로 만들어 주셨다.)

(3) S + vt + O + O.C(현재분사·과거분사)

·I saw him kissing his lover.

(나는 그가 그의 애인과 키스하는 것을 보았다.)

·I heard my name called behind me.

(나는 나의 이름이 등 뒤에서 불려지는 것을 들었다.)

(4) S + vt + O + O.C(to부정사)

·She advised me to go there.

(그녀는 나에게 거기에 가는 것이 좋겠다고 말했다.)

(5) S + vt + O + (to be) + 명사·형용사

·I consider him (to be) a fool [very foolish].

(나는 그를 바보라고[매우 바보스럽다고]생각한다.)

(6) S + vt + O + as + O.C

·I consider her as my best friend[very kind].

(나는 그녀가 나의 가장 좋은 친구라고[매우 친절하다고]생각한다.)

(7) S + vt + it + O.C + 명사구(절)

(가목적어) (진목적어)

to tell a lie. 〈부정사〉

·I think it wrong

telling a lie. 〈동명사〉

(나는 거짓말하는 것은 나쁘다고 생각합니다.)

·I think it wrong that she got it.
(나는 그녀가 그것을 취한 것은 부당하다고 생각한다.)

◈ **불완전타동사**: 타동사는 목적어를 그 뒤에 받아서 문장을 완성시키는데, 어떤 타동사는 그 뒤에 목적어를 취해도 술부를 완성시킬 수 없어서 다시 보어(Complement)를 필요로 하는 동사가 있다. 이러한 성질의 동사를 불완전타동사라 하고 그 보어를 목적격보어(Objective Complement)라 한다.

◈ **목적어와 목적보어와의 관계**: 목적어의 성질과 상태(또는 동작)를 보충 설명하는 것이 목적보어의 역할인데 그 앞에 있는 목적어와는 주술관계를 이룬다. 즉, 의미상으로 「O + O.C」는 「S'+ V'」의 관계를 이룬다는 것이다.

①

S + vt + O + O.C
= (S + V) + (O + O.C)
= (S + V) + (S' + V')

·I found the book easy.
(S) (vt) (O) (O.C)
= (I found) (the book easy.)
= (I found) that (the book was easy.)
(S) (V) (S') (V')

C 제 5문형 익히기 Basic Sentence Drill

a. Mr. William
a teacher
honest

b. Linda Kim
a nurse
dedicated

c. Miss Chun
a secretary
capable

d. Miss Yang
a radio announcer
versatile

e. Robert Schuller
a computer specialist
brilliant

f. Albert Chung
a journalist
interesting

예) a. Mr. William is a teacher, and I think of him honest.

b. ______________________________

c. ______________________________

d. ______________________________

e. ______________________________

f. ______________________________

D 응용 영작 Advanced Composition

Level 1

① 나는 그녀를 엄마라고 불렀다.

: I called her 'Mama.'

② 그들은 Mr. Kim을 자기들의 지도자로 선출했다.

:

③ 우리 교회는 그를 *당회장 목사님으로 *결의했다.

:

Level 2

① *총사령관은 부하들에게 *공격하라고 *명령했다.

:

② 우리는 우리의 인생이 *무상하다고 생각한다.

:

③ 나는 그가 어떤 사람을 *때리고 있는 것을 보았다.

:

Level 3

① *합의가 되어 일의 재개가 가능해졌다.

:

② 그가 그렇게 멋진 차를 운전하는 것을 상상할 수 있습니까?

:

③ *6·25동란은 한국의 *주요 도시를 *폐허로 남겨놓았다.

:

▸ **Word Tips for composition**

* 당회장 목사님: a senior pastor
* 결의하다: decide
* 총사령관: The Commander in Chief
* 명령하다: command, give an order to
* 공격하다: attack
* 무상하다: futile, meaningless, vain
* 합의: agreement, settlement
* 때리다: beat
* 6·25 동란: Korean War
* 주요 도시: the major cities
* 폐허로 남겨놓다: leave ~ a ruin

O O.C

E 응용 독해문 Applied Passages

Scientists are always trying out new ways of growing food, but even they can only guess what food will be like in the future.

You can perhaps get a better focus on what lies ahead from the four ideas below.

Read them and see if you can guess what the future hamburger will taste like.

The sea can be farmed.

Only one third of the earth's area is land.

The reminder is sea.

The ocean contains huge amounts of tiny sea-animals called krill.

Krill are already in some fish products, such as fish sticks and canned crab.

Next time you buy canned or frozen seafood look carefully at the label.

You might see krill listed as one of the ingredients.

Seaweed is another source of future food from the ocean.

It is used in ice cream and some breads.

Animals can be changed.

A farmer is able to “engineer” his animals by adding hormones to their feed.

Hormones can make chicken meat more tender or beef less fat.

For example, dairy farmers add growth hormones so that calves produce milk sooner than normal.

New crops can be planted.

Today, rice supports more than half the world's population.

F 5형식 관련 성경 표현 Related Expression in the Bible

① Acts 13:47(사도행전 13:47)

"I have made you a light for *Gentiles that you may bring salvation to the ends of the earth."

(내가 너를 이방의 빛을 삼아 너로 땅 끝까지 구원하게 하리라)

* Gentiles: 이방, 이방인

② John 1:38(요한복음 1:38)

Turning around, Jesus saw them following and asked, "What do you want?"

(예수께서 돌이켜 그 좇는 것을 보시고 물어 가라사대, "무엇을 구하느냐?")

③ Genesis 41:15(창세기 41:15)

But I have heard it said of you that when you hear a dream you can interpret it.

(들은즉, 너는 꿈을 들으면 능히 푼다하더라.)

④ I Thessalonians 3:1(데살로니가전서 3:1)

So when we could *stand it no longer, we thought it best to be left by ourselves in Athens.

(이러므로 우리가 참다 못하여 우리가 아덴에 머물기를 좋게 여겨)

* stand: 참다. persist, put up with

→ stand no longer 더 이상 참지 못하다

⑤ Deuteronomy 5:11(신명기 5:11)

"You shall not misuse the name of the Lord your God, for the Lord will not *hold anyone *guiltless(who misuses his name.)

(너는 너의 하나님 여호와의 이름을 망령되이 일컫지 말라. 나 여호와는 나의 이름을 망령되이 일컫는 자를 죄 없는 줄로 인정치 아니하리라.)

* hold: 여기다. 인정하다(regard, approve, acknowledge)

선교
영어
회화

English For Mission

CHAPTER II

영어의 12가지 시제 중 기본 시제 이용 말하기:

단순현재; 단순과거; 단순미래

Lesson 6

A good man obtains favor from the LORD, but the LORD condemns a crafty man.

단순현재(Simple Present Tense) 문장 이용

A 성경 독해 NIV Reading

Proverbs 12:1-5

1 Whoever loves discipline loves knowledge, but he who hates correction is stupid.

2 A good man obtains favor from the LORD, but the LORD condemns a crafty man.

3 A man cannot be established through wickedness, but the righteous cannot be uprooted.

4 A wife of noble character is her husband's crown, but a disgraceful wife is like decay in his bones.

5 The plans of the righteous are just, but the advice of the wicked is deceitful.

한글성경 참조

잠언 12:1–5

1 훈계를 좋아하는 자는 지식을 좋아하거니와 징계를 싫어하는 자는 짐승과 같으니라

2 선인은 여호와께 은총을 받으려니와 악을 꾀하는 자는 정죄하심을 받으리라

3 사람이 악으로서 굳게 서지 못하거니와 의인의 뿌리는 움직이지 아니하느니라

4 어진 여인은 그 지아비의 면류관이나 욕을 끼치는 여인은 그 지아비의 뼈가 썩음 같게
하느니라

5 의인의 생각은 정직하여도 악인의 도모는 속임이니라

B 단순현재(Simple Sentence) 문장 익히기 Basic Sentence Drill

1. What are your weekend hobbies?

① I play baseball with my friend every Saturday.

②

③

④

⑤

2. What are your own personality traits?

Please check the ones that are true about you and check also the simple present tense verb by underlining it.

1. ☐ I bite nails when I'm embarrassed.
2. ☐ I often talk to myself.
3. ☐ I'm impatient.
4. ☐ I like things organized.
5. ☐ I'm always on time.
6. ☐ I get frustrated easily.
7. ☐ I have a good sense of humor.
8. ☐ I fall in love with someone too easily.emotion.
9. ☐ I'm very emotional.
10. ☐ I'm easy to be pleased.
11. ☐ I'm a good listener.
12. ☐ I'm inconsistent.
13. ☐ I get along well with people.
14. ☐ I worry too much about my appearance.
15. ☐ I always keep my promise.
16. ☐ I get stressed out easily.
17. ☐ I laugh too loud.
18. ☐ I'm very well balanced in my
19. ☐ I often lose my temper.
20. ☐ I don't exercise regularly.

C 관련문법 Related Grammar Review

영어회화를 잘 하는 비결 중 한 가지는 동사의 시제(Tense)를 정확하게 구사하는 일이다. 한국어와 달리 영어는 시간 표현, 즉 기본시제의 3가지인 현재(present)·과거(part)·미래(Future)에 상당히 민감하여 아무리 구어체(spoken English) 표현이라 하더라도 시제부분에 대하여는 엄격한 정확성을 요구하고 있다. 각 기본 시제별로 진행시제, 완료시제, 완료진행시제로 다시 세분되며 결국 총 12가지 시제로 구분되어 쓰여진다. 그 중 이번 과에서는 단순 현재(simple present tense)의 용법만 구분하여 익혀보기로 하자. 단순현재는 밑의 도표에서 알 수 있듯이 또 다시 현재진행시제(be + ing), 현재완료시제(have, has + p·p), 현재완료진행(has, have been + ~ing)시제와 그 용법이나 형식이 구분되지만, 이 단순현재시제에는 동사의 기본 형태만 쓰여진다.

다음 요약한 도표로 구분하여 보자.

기본시제	현재 + ⑤ → 현재시제(V~)
	과거 + ⑤ → 과거시제(V(e)d~
	현재 + ① + ⑤ → 미래시제(will·shall + V(be)~)
진행시제	현재 + ③ → 현재진행시제(am. are, is + ~ing)
	과거 + ③ → 과거진행시제(was, were + ~ing)
	현재 + ① + ③ → 미래진행시제(will, shall be + ~ing)
완료시제	현재 + ② → 현재완료시제(have, has + p·p)
	과거 + ② → 과거완료시제(had + p·p)
	현재 + ① + ② → 미래완료시제(will, shall have + p·p)
완료진행 시제	현재 + ② + ③ → 현재완료진행시제(have, has been + ~ing)
	과거 + ② + ③ → 과거완료진행시제(had been + ~ing)
	현재 + ① + ② + ③ → 미래완료진행시제(will, shall have been + ~ing)

* ④ 번은 12시제(능동형)를 수동형 * 미래형시제도 현재시제의 일종으로 취급한다.

▣ 현재시제(Present Tense):

(1) 현재의 사실(현재의 동작과 상태)

·We live in the suburbs.

(우리는 근교에 살고 있다.)

·There comes a bus.

(저기 버스가 온다.)

(2) 현재의 습관적인 행위

·I get up at six in the morning.

(나는 아침 6시에 일어난다.)

·I go to church every sundays.

(나는 매주 일요일이면 교회에 (예배드리러) 간다.)

(3) 직업 또는 그와 같이 늘 하는 행위

·I teach English in the school. 〈직업〉

(나는 학교에서 영어를 가르친다 - 영어선생이다.)

·My daughter goes to school. 〈늘 하는 행위〉

(나의 딸은 학교에 (공부하러) 다닌다.)

·She sings very well. (= She is a good singer.)

(그녀는 노래를 잘 부른다 - 가수이다.)

[주의] 위에서 그녀는 지금 노래 부르고 있는 것이 아니라 직업으로서의 문제인 것이다. 만일 어떤 여자가 단순히 노래 부르고 있는 중이라면 "She is singing now"라고 해야 된다.

(4) 변함없는 진리·속담

·The earth moves round the sun. 〈진리〉

(지구는 태양 주위를 돈다.)

·The early bird catches the worm. 〈속담〉

(일찍 나오는 새가 벌레를 잡는다.)

(5) 옛 저서(성현의 말)의 인용

·Dryden says that none but the brave deserve(s) the fair.

("용기있는 자만이 미인을 얻을 자격이 있다"고 드라이든은 말한다.)

·Pascal says, "Man is a thinking reed."

("인간은 생각하는 갈대"라고 파스칼은 말한다.)

(6) 미래시제의 대용(代用)

미래를 나타내는 시간부사(구)와 함께 쓰인 왕래발착의 동사들.

〔go, come, start, leave, arrive, return, sail, ride, depart, meet, reach,…개시(being), 종료(finish) …〕

·He returns next weekend.

(= He will return next weekend)

(그는 다음 주말에 돌아 올 겁니다.)

·Professor Lee retires next year. 〈종료〉

(= Professor Lee will retire next year.)

(이 교수님께서는 다음 해에 퇴직하시게 된다.)

Exercise

Please complete the sentences with proper forms of verbs.

맞는 동사 형태로 공란을 채우시오.

1. My cousin is an architect.
   He designs a plan(project) for buildings.
   * lay out / draw up의 숙어를 써도 됨: (도면)을 설계하다.

2. Ms. Cho is a hair dresser. She ______ hair for everybody who comes into the shop.

3. My father is a veterinarian. He __________ care of all the animals if there is something wrong.

4. Yoshimoto is a salesclerk. He __________ products to people.

5. My mother is a full-time housekeeper. She __________ dinner three times a day.

6. Mr. Young is a delivery person. He __________ the parcels to all my neighbors, including me.

7. Soon Hee is a receptionist. She __________ all the telephone calls everyday during office hours.

8. My niece is a flight attendant. She people in the flight and also __________ food every meal time.

9. Chul Soo is a pharmacist. He __________drugs for patients.

10. Bill is a mechanic. He can __________ the broken things.

11. His Dad is a travel agent. He __________ the trips for people with all different purposes.

12. They are business people. They __________ the goods to overseas by doing import and export.

D 응용 영작 Advanced Composition

단순현재동사 사용

Level 1

① 우리 가족은 주말마다 *등산갑니다.

:

② 우리 이웃은 (옆집은) 토요일마다 야외에 나가서 *사진을 찍습니다.

:

Level 2

① 내 친구는 *속상할 때 *손톱을 뜯습니다.

:

② 우리 아버지는 매일 밤 *코를 고십니다.

:

Level 3

① *경상남도의 *특산물은 사과입니다.

:

② 다이어트를 오래 계속한다는 것은 어렵습니다.

:

③ 우리 학교는 ABC컨트리 클럽에서 *서너 블록 정도 *떨어져 있습니다.

:

▸ **Word Tips for composition**

* 등산가다: go mountain climbing
* 사진찍다: take pictures
* 속상하다: be frustrated
* 손톱을 뜯다: bite one's nails
* 코골다: snore
* 경상남도: the southern province of KyungSang
* 서너 블록 정도: about three or four blocks
* 떨어져 있다: be ~ away from

E 응용 독해문 Applied Passages

The Gospels are our most important source of information about Jesus Christ.

They are primarily testimonies of faith used in early Christian preaching.

Their purpose is not to give a complete picture of the life of Jesus; these records of His words and acts are designed, rather, to demonstrate as well founded apostolic proclamation that Jesus is Christ and Lord.

They propose to show that the faith of the Church and its comprehension of the person of Jesus go back to Jesus Himself.

F 관련 성경 표현 Related Expression in the Bible

Psalms 1:1-4, 6(시편 1:1-4, 6)

1절 ① Blessed is the man who does not walk in the counsel of the wicked or stand in the way of sinners or sit in the seat of mockers.

(복 있는 자는 악인의 꾀를 좇지 아니하며 죄인의 길에 서지 아니하며 오만한 자의 자리에 앉지 아니하고)

2절 ② But his delight is in the law of the Lord, and on his law he meditates day and night.

(오직 여호와의 율법을 즐거워하며 그 율법 주야로 묵상하는 자로다.)

3절 ③ He is like a tree planted by streams of water, which yields its fruit in season and whose leaf does not wither. Whatever he does prospers.

(저는 시냇가에 심은 나무가 시절을 좇아 과실을 맺으며 그 잎사귀가 마르지 아니함 같으니 그 행사가 다 형통하리로다.)

4절 ④ Not so the wicked! They are like chaff the wind blows away.

(악인은 그렇지 않음이여 오직 바람에 나는 겨와 같도다.)

6절 ⑤ For the Lord watches over the way of the righteous, but the way of the wicked will perish.

(대저 의인의 길은 여호와께서 인정하시나 악인의 길은 망하리로다.)

Free Talking Assignment

다음 시간을 나타내는 부사구를 사용하여 보통 규칙적 또는 습관적으로 하는 생활행위를 Free Talking 해 오도록 하자.

예) ① very early in the morning →

My mother gets up very early in the morning to attend early morning chapel at 5 o'clock.

② in the morning →

③ at noon →

④ in the afternoon →

⑤ in the evening →

⑥ at night →

⑦ in the middle of the night →

⑧ at daybreak →

⑨ at dusk(in the dusk of evening) →

⑩ from dawn till dusk →

Lesson 7

As evening approached, there came a rich man from Arimathea, named Joseph.

단순과거(Simple Past Tense) 문장 이용

A 성경 독해 NIV Reading

Matthew 27:57-60

57 As evening approached, there came a rich man from Arimathea,
named Joseph, who had himself become a disciple of Jesus.
58 Going to Pilate, he asked for Jesus' body, and Pilate ordered that
it be given to him.
59 Joseph took the body, wrapped it in a clean linen cloth,
60 and placed it in his own new tomb that he had cut out of the rock.
He rolled a big stone in front of the entrance to the tomb and
went away.

한글성경 참조

마태 27:57-60

57저물었을 때에 아리마대의 부자 요셉이라 하는 사람이 왔으니 그도 예수의 제자라

58빌라도에게 가서 예수의 시체를 달라 하니 이에 빌라도가 내주라 명령하거늘

59요셉이 시체를 가져다가 깨끗한 세마포로 싸서

60바위 속에 판 자기 새 무덤에 넣어 두고 큰 돌을 굴려 무덤 문에 놓고 가니

단순과거 시제 말하기 연습

(Please fill in the blanks with proper past form of verbs.)

I ________ born in 1984 in Seoul. I ________ up in a comparatively large family, members of 9. We ________ to go to the same church and ________ vacation together for summer season. Our relatives ________ come to us to spend time together. Even though we ________ not rich family we ________ happy. Whenever we ________ difficulty we ________ together to God and he ________ us the answer. If we ________ rich we ________ not depend upon God as much as we should.

B 관련 문법 Related Grammar Review

과거시제 용법

(1) 과거의 사실(과거의 동작과 상태)

·I got up at six this morning.

(나는 오늘 아침 6시에 일어났다.)

·They fell in love at first sight.

(그들은 첫눈에 사랑에 빠졌다.)

(2) 과거의 습관: 규칙적인 습관(used to + 동사원형~)

·불규칙적인 습관(would + 동사원형~) 또는 과거시간부사 "often, every~" 등을 이용하기도 한다.

·I got up at six every mitning.

(나는 매일 아침 6시에 일어났다.)

·I met her very often during my staying in Seoul.

(나는 서울에 체류하고 있는 동안 그녀를 자주 만나곤 했다.)

·She would often come to meet me. 〈가끔 ~하곤 했다.〉

(그녀는 나를 만나기 위해 자주 〈그러나 가끔〉 오곤 했다.)

·She used to be cheerful in her schooldays. 〈계속~하곤 했다.〉

(그녀는 학창시절에는 명랑하였다.)

(3) 역사적 사실은 아무리 오래 되었어도 과거시제를 쓴다.

·Columbus discovered America in 1492.

(콜럼버스는 1492년에 미국을 발견했다.)

·World war II broke out in 1939.

(세계 제2차 대전은 1939년에 발발했다.)

(4) 과거동사에「never, ever」를 수반하면 과거의 경험(현재까지의 경험)을 나타낸다. 즉, 현재완료(경험)를 대신한 표현이다.

·I never saw(= have never seen) such a beauty.

(나는 그런 미인을 본 경험이 없다.)

·Did you ever see such a beauty?

(= Have you ever seen such a beauty?)

(당신은 이제껏 그런 미인을 본 경험이 있습니까?)

(5) 시간의 접속사와 함께 쓰여 시간의 전·후 관계가 명백할 때 〈과거완료 대용〉

·She suddenly felt hungry after she cried(= had cried).

(그녀는 운 다음 갑자기 배가 고픈 것을 느꼈다.)

·As soon as she saw(had seen) me, she ran away.

(그녀는 나를 보자마자 곧바로 도망쳤다.)

[주의] ·He thought that he was a genius.

(그는 자신이 천재라고 생각하고 있었다.)

→ 종속절의 동사가 과거형이더라도 현재시제처럼 해석하는 경우이다.

·If I were rich, I could buy the car.

(= As I am not rich, I can't buy the car.)

→ 가정절 속의 과거형 were의 형태는 과거형이지만 그 뜻은 현재형임에 주의해야 된다.

C 단순과거 문장 익히기 Basic Sentence Drill

Tell me about your last wedding anniversary(or birthday).

1. What did you do?

   We ______________________________

2. Did you give your wife a gift?

   Yes, ______________________________

3. What did you get from your wife?(or husband)

   ____

4. Did your family and friends do anything special for you?

   Yes, my family ______________________________

   and my friends ______________________________

D 응용 영작 Advanced Composition

Simple past tense

Level 1

① 그녀는 집에 늦게 도착했다. 그래서 배가 고팠다.

:

② 나는 *입맛을 잃었다. 그래서 저녁을 많이 먹을 수가 없었다.

:

③ 우리 선생님은 *약 한두 해 전에 교통사고를 당했다.
그래서 *왼쪽 팔이 부러졌다.

:

Level 2

① 한국동란은 1950년에 *발발했다.

:

② 나는 대학시절에 그녀와 *연애했다.

:

Level 3

① 한국사회가 *유교적이라는 것은 *아주 당연한 일이다(It ~that 사용).

:

② '양반'이란 *사회계급은 문자적으로는 결국 *특권층을 의미했다.

:

▸ **Word Tips for composition**

* 입맛을 잃다: lose one's appetite
* 약 한두 해전에: about a couple of years ago
* 왼쪽 팔이 부러지다: have a left arm broken
* 발발하다: break out
* 연애하다: fall in love with 人(사상, 물건)~
* 유교적: Confucian
* 아주 당연하다: be quite natural
* 사회계급: social hierarchy
* 특권층: the priviliged(the underprivileged)

E 응용 독해문 Applied Passage

At the age of six, I left my parents to be adopted to one of my father's male cousins.

From that time on, I was doomed to a lonely lift far away from my parents and other brothers and sisters.

When I was twenty-one years old, I began to worry about my future life.

Finally I decided that I could not help the problems of my life.

But, I happened to attend a church in the spring when I was twenty- four.

At the age of twenty-five, I was baptized.

However, my Christian life brought devout followers of persecution from the family.

Traditionally our family enjoyed ancestor worship.

Because I was an adopted son to my childless relatives, my opposition to their ancestor worship became a very serious matter.

Under those circumstances, I was disowned by my foster family, just as I had expected …

F 관련 성경 표현 Related Expression in the Bible

① Genesis 1:1(창세기 1:1)

In the beginning, God created the heavens and the earth.

(태초에 하나님이 천지를 창조하시니라.)

② Ezra 2:63(에스라 2:63)

The *governor ordered them not to eat any of *the most sacred food until there was a priest ministering with and Urim and Thummim.

(방백이 저희에게 명하여 우림과 둔밈을 가진 제사장이 일어나기 전에는 지성물을 먹지 말라 하였느니라.)

* governor: 방백, (現)주지사.
* the most sacred food: 지성물

③ Mark 9:25(마가복음 9:25)

When Jesus saw that *a crowed was running to *the scene, he rebuked the *evil spirit.

(예수께서 무리의 달려 모이는 것을 보시고 그 더러운 귀신을 꾸짖어 가라사대)

* a crowd: (귀신의) 무리 = multitude
* run to the scene: (현장으로) 달려 모이다
* evil spirit: 더러운 귀신(dirty spirit)

④ Mark 9:26(마가복음 9:26)

The spirit *shrieked, *convulsed him violently and came out. The boy looked so much like a corpse that many said, "He's dead."

(귀신이 소리지르며 아이로 심히 경련을 일으키게 하고 나가니 그 아이가 죽은 것같이 되어 많은 사람이 말하기를 죽었다 하나)

* shriek: 소리지르다(비명따위) = scream
* convulse: 경련(소란)을 일으키다. convulsion

⑤ john 5:45(요한복음 5:45)

When he arrived in Galilee, the Galileans welcomed him.

(갈릴리에 이르시매 갈릴리인들이 그를 영접하였다.)

Lesson 8

I will shake all nations, and the desired of all nations will come, and I will fill this house with glory.

단순미래(Simple Future Tense) 문장 이용

A 성경 독해 NIV Reading

Haggai 2:6-9

6 "This is what the LORD Almighty says: 'In a little while I will
once more shake the heavens and the earth, the sea and the dry
land.

7 I will shake all nations, and the desired of all nations will come,
and I will fill this house with glory,' says the LORD Almighty.

8 'The silver is mine and the gold is mine,' declares the LORD
Almighty.

9 'The glory of this present house will be greater than the glory of
the former house,' says the LORD Almighty. 'And in this place I
will grant peace,' declares the LORD Almighty."

한글성경 참조

학개 2:6-9

6 만군의 여호와가 이같이 말하노라 조금 있으면 내가 하늘과 땅과 바다와 육지를 진동
시킬 것이요

7 또한 모든 나라를 진동시킬 것이며 모든 나라의 보배가 이르리니 내가 이 성전에 영광
이 충만하게 하리라 만군의 여호와의 말이니라

8 은도 내 것이요 금도 내 것이니라 만군의 여호와의 말이니라

9 이 성전의 나중 영광이 이전 영광보다 크리라 만군의 여호와의 말이니라 내가 이곳에
평강을 주리라 만군의 여호와의 말이니라

B 관련문법 Related Grammar Review

미래시제는 「will(또는 shall)+동사원형」의 형식으로 나타내는데, 사람의 의지와 상관없이 어떤 일이 자연의 추세에 따라 일어나게 되는 「단순미래」와 앞으로 일어날 일이 사람의 의지에 따라 일어나게 되는 「의지 미래」의 두 가지로 미래시제는 나누어진다.

	단 순 미 래		의 지 미 래	
	평서문 (~할 것이다)	의문문 (~할 것인가?)	평서문 (화자의 의지)	의문문(상대방의 의지를 물음)
1인칭	I(We) shall~ (미, will)	Shall I(We)~? (미, will)	I(We) will ~ (~하겠다)	Shall I(We)~? (~할까요?)
2인칭	You(단·복)	will~Will you (단·복)~? (영, shall)	You(단·복수)shall~ (~하게 하겠다)	Will you(단·복)~? (~해 주시겠습니까?)
3인칭	He(She, It, 복수, They)	Will he (she, it, 복수 they)~?	He(She, It, 복수 They) shall ~(~하게 하겠다)	Shall he(she, it, 복수 they)~? (~하게 할까요?)

[주의] ⓐ 의지미래: You shall ~: 너에게 ~하게 하겠다.

He(She, It, They)shall~: 그(그녀, 그것, 그들)에게 ~하게 하겠다.

Shall he(She, It, They)shall~: 그(그녀, 그것, 그들)에게 ~하게 할까요?

ⓑ 현대영어에서는 뜻·용법 모두에서 「will」로 통일되어 가고 있다.

단순미래 1인칭에서 영국식은 shall이지만, 미국식은 will을 쓴다.

ⓒ 「be going to~」: "~할 것이다, ~할 예정(작정)이다"라는 뜻으로 미래의 예정이나 의지를 나타내며 구어에서 will, shall을 대신한다.

·I shall(will) be thirty years old next year. 〈단순미래〉

(= I am going to be thirty years old next year.)

(다음 해가 되면 나는 30살이 될 것이다.)

·Shall(Will) I get well soon? 〈단순미래〉

(내가 곧 건강해 질까요?)

·I will fo there. 〈의지미래(화자의 의지)〉

(= I am going to go there)

(나는 그 곳에 가겠다.)

·You shall be in higher position, if you work hard. 〈의지미래(화자의 의지)〉

(= I will give you a high position, if you work harder.)

(열심히 일을 한다면, 너를 높은 지위에 앉게 하겠다.)

·She shall send you some money. 〈의지미래(화자의 의지)〉

(= I will make her send you some money.)

(그녀에게 약간의 돈을 당신께 보내도록 하겠다.)

·Shall my daughter go first? 〈의지미래(상대의 의지)〉

(= Do you want me to let my daughter go first?)

(제 딸에게 먼저 가라고 할까요?)

C 단순미래 문장 익히기 Basic Sentence Drill

Please fill in the blanks

1. Will the opera begin pretty soon? Yes, it ______________.

   It'll ______________ in a couple of minutes.

2. Miss Kim is recovered now. She'll __________ __________ of the hospital __________ a few days.

3. Will it be cold tomorrow? Probably, __________ __________.

   It'll __________ cold tomorrow and __________ be as hot as today.

4. The train'll arrive in any minute. Don't miss it! OK. I'll __________ ready to get on in a little while.

5. I'm sure __________ will rain tomorrow.

6. I bet it __________ get warm this afternoon.

7. It'll be spring. It __________ snow any more and we __________ have to stayindoors anymore.

D 응용 영작 Advanced Composition

Level 1

① Mr. Kim은 몇 년 내에 *승진될 것이다.

:

② Miss Kim은 십 년 후에 아기 엄마가 될 것이다.

:

Level 2

① 그녀는 부자가 되면 *자선사업을 많이 할 것이다.

:

② 내가 비록 잘못할지라도 우리 엄마는 내게 *소리치지 않을 것이다.

:

Level 3

① 한국원화의 *환율이 곧 *폭등할 것이다.

:

② 남한과 북한의 정부가 잘 협조하면 평화로운 통일을 기대할 수 있을 것이다.

:

▸ **Word Tips for composition**

* 승진되다: be promoted
* 자선사업하다: do the charitable work
* 소리치다: yell at
* 환율: the rate of exchange
* 폭등하다: shoot up

E 응용 독해문 Applied Passages

Today we'll talk about the future world.

Have you ever thought about the future world?

Let's say, in 2020, will the world be much better than it is now?

What do you think, In-Su?

Well, I think the world will be much better.

Medical science will help people enjoy good health and long life.

Maybe you're right, but we must think of the other side also.

First of all, the world will be overcrowded with people.

The population problem is serious.

The world will be short of food, oil, and other natural resources.

I think Mi-Ae is right. Many people are starving now, and more people will be hungry in the future.

And air and water pollution will be worse because the numbers of cars and people are increasing rapidly.

Let's look in the bright side.

You don't need to worry if you believe in science.

Perhaps science will solve almost all problems in the future.

For example, people will be using electric or solar energy cars in the future.

Factories and houses will be using new types of energy.

Then we won't have air pollution on the earth any longer.

F 관련 성경표현 Related Expression in Bible

① Matthew 16:19(마태복음 16:19)

I will give you the keys of the kingdom of heaven; whatever you bind on earth will be bound in heaven, and whatever you loose on earth will be loosed in heaven.

(내가 천국열쇠를 네게 주리니 네가 땅에서 무엇이든지 매면 하늘에서도 매일 것이요, 네가 땅에서 무엇이든지 풀면 하늘에서도 풀리리라.)

② Habakkuk 2:11(하박국 2:11)

The stones of the wall will cry out and the beams of the woodwork will echo it.

(담에서 돌이 부르짖고 집에서 들보가 응답하리라.)

③ I Samuel 1:11(사무엘상 1:11)

__________, Then I will give him to the Lord for all the days of his life, and no *razor will ever be used on his head.

(~하시면, 내가 그의 평생에 그를 여호와께 드리고 삭도를 그 머리에 대지 아니하겠나이다.)

* razor 삭도, 면도칼

④ Malachi 1:11(말라기 1:11)

My name will be great among the nations *from the rising to the setting of the sun.

(해뜨는 곳에서부터 해지는 곳까지의 이방 민족 중에서 내 이름이 크게 될 것이라.)

* from the rising to the setting of the sun: 해 뜨는 곳에서부터 해지는 곳까지의.

⑤ I Timothy 4:1(디모데전서 4:1)

The Spirit clearly says that in later times some will abandon the faith and follow *deceiving spirits and things taught by *demons.
(그러나 성령이 밝히 말씀하시기를 후일에 어떤 사람들이 믿음에서 떠나 미혹케 하는 영과 귀신의 가르침을 좇으리라 하셨으니.)

* deceiving spirits: 미혹케 하는 영
* demons: 귀신

Free Talking Assignment

Please share your future project for 10years from now.

① In the year of 2001, I will (am going to) prepare for driving test to get the license.

② In 2005, ______________________________

③ In 2006, ______________________________

④ In 2007, ______________________________

⑤ In 2008, ______________________________

⑥ In 2009, ______________________________

⑦ In 2010, ______________________________

선교 영어 회화

English For Mission

CHAPTER III

여러 가지 조동사 이용 말하기

Lesson 9

I would march against them in battle; I would set them all on fire.

여러 가지 조동사(Auxiliary Verbs) 이용

A 성경 독해 NIV Reading

Isaiah 27:3-6

3 I, the LORD, watch over it; I water it continually. I guard it day
and night so that no one may harm it.

4 I am not angry. If only there were briers and thorns confronting
me! I would march against them in battle; I would set them all
on fire.

5 Or else let them come to me for refuge; let them make peace
with me, yes, let them make peace with me."

6 In days to come Jacob will take root, Israel will bud and blossom
and fill all the world with fruit.

한글성경 참조

이사야 27:3-6

3 나 여호와는 포도원지기가 됨이여 때때로 물을 주며 밤낮으로 간수하여 아무든지 이
를 해치지 못하게 하리로다
4 나는 포도원에 대하여 노함이 없나니 찔레와 가시가 나를 대적하여 싸운다 하자 내가
그것을 밟고 모아 불사르리라
5 그리하지 아니하면 내 힘을 의지하고 나와 화친하며 나와 화친할 것이니라
6 후일에는 야곱의 뿌리가 박히며 이스라엘의 움이 돋고 꽃이 필 것이라 그들이 그 결실
로 지면을 채우리로다

B 관련문법 Related Grammar Review

여러 가지 조동사(Auxiliary Verbs)

조동사는 반드시 동사에 수반되어 그 동사를 여러 가지 뜻으로 보충해 주는 역할을 하는데 「의문문, 부정문, 시제, 태」를 나타내는 데도 중요한 역할을 한다. 그리고 반드시 본동사의 바로 앞에 놓인다.

1. 조동사의 종류

	현재형	과거형	용법
조동사와 본동사 양쪽으로 쓸 수 있는 것들	am·are·is	was·were	진행형·수동형에서
	have·has	had	완료형에서
	do·does	did	의문·부정·강조문에서
	need		~할 필요가 있다
	dare	dared	감히 ~하다
조동사로만 쓸 수 있는 것들	will	would	미래시제로서
	shall	should	특별용법이 있다
	can	could	~할 수 있다
	may	might	~해도 좋다 ~일지도 모른다
	must	had(to)	~해야 된다 ~임에 틀림없다
	ought(to)		~해야 된다 ~임에 틀림없다
		used(to)	늘 ~하곤 했다

* 조동사 뒤에 또 다른 조동사를 계속 쓸 수 없음에 주의해야 된다. 그리고 문장 주어의 시제·수를 동사 대신 받는다.

I am staying at my friend's house.

This letter was written by my friend in London.

She has finished reading the book.

He did not go there yesterday.

She speaks(spoke) English well.
She can(could) speak English well.

2. 조동사의 용법

(1) 「be·do·have」

be동사는 「진행형과 수동태」를 만들 때의 be동사를 말하며, do동사는 「의문문·부정문·강조형식·앞서 나온 동사를 받는 경우」를 말하며, 그리고 have동사는 「완료형」에서 사용된 경우이다.

·It is raining now.
(지금 비가 내리고 있다.)
·English is spoken in Australia.
(호주에서는 영어가 사용되고 있다.)
·He has lost his new watch.
(그는 새 시계를 잃어버렸다.)
·Do you watch television? - Yes, I do.
(TV를 보고 있습니까? - 예, 그렇습니다.)
·The prophecy did come true.
(그 예언은 정말 들어맞았다.)
·I like lemons. - So do I.(= I like lemons, too.)
(나는 레몬을 좋아합니다. - 나 또한 그렇습니다.)
* I do not like lemons. - Nor(Neither) do I.(I don't like lemons, either.)
·Never did I see such a pretty girl. 〈도치문〉
(그렇게 예쁜 소녀를 본 적이 없다.)

(2) 「will, shall」

will, shall이 미래시제로 쓰이는 경우에는 단순미래와 의지미래로 구분되어 사용된다(이미 앞서 설명한 바 있으므로 생략). 그러나 그 외의 용법으로도 자주 사용되기 때문에 주의해야 되는데 will은 「현재의 추측, 고집과 거절, 습성과 경향, 현재의 습관」으로 사용되고, shall은 「법률·규칙·예언·계율」 등으로 사용된다.

·He will often forget his promise. 〈현재의 습관〉
(그는 약속을 자주 잊는다.)

·A tiger will attack people when his hungry. 〈습성〉
(호랑이는 흔히 배가 고플 때 사람에게 달려든다.)

·This book will be hers. 〈현재의 추측〉
(이 책은 그녀의 것 같다.)

·The door will not open. 〈고집, 거절〉
(〈아무리 시도를 해 봐도〉 그 문은 열리지 않는다.)

·Freedom of speech shall not be violated. 〈법률, 규칙〉
(언론의 자유는 보장된다.)

·Ask, and it shall be given you. 〈예언, 계율〉
(구하라, 그리하면 얻을 것이다.)

(3) 「should, would(used to)」

① should의 용법

·You should be kind to old people. 〈의무, 당연〉
(노인에게 친절해야 한다.)

·He insisted that I should make a speech.
(그는 내가 연설을 해야 한다고 주장했다.)

[주의] 명령·제안·요구·결정·동의·고집·소망의 동사가 이끄는 that 절 속에 「should + 동·원~」이 쓰인다.

·It is strange that she should go to such a place.
(그녀가 그러한 장소에 갔다는 것은 이상하다.)
·It is natural that she should come.
(그녀가 온 것은 당연하다.)

[주의] 「It + be + 감정·이성적 판단의 형용사 + that + S'+ should + 동·원」의 형식이다.

·I hurried to the station lest I should miss the train.
(= I hurried to the station so that I might not miss the train.)
(나는 기차를 놓치지 않으려고 서둘러서 정류장으로 갔다.)
·I should(or would) like to call on you today. 〈정중한 표현〉
(오늘 당신을 찾아 뵈었으면 합니다.)
·How should I know the fact? 〈수사의문문〉
(내가 그 사실을 어떻게 알겠느냐?)
·Who should come in but the man himself? 〈의외의 놀람〉
(누가 들어오는가 했더니 다름아닌 바로 그 사람이었다.)

[주의] should가 의문사 등과 함께 쓰여 뜻밖의 놀람 표시나 알 수 없겠다는 뜻을 나타내는 경우도 있다.

② would, used to의 용법
·He who would search of pearls must dive deep.
〈현재의 희망·강한 의지〉
(= wishes to)

(진주를 찾으려는 자는 깊이 잠수해야 한다.)

·They would start sailing, though we told them not to. 〈과거의 고집과 거절〉

(우리가 항해를 하면 안된다 했을지라도 기어코 그들은 항해를 떠났다.)

·Would you write your name in my notebook? 〈정중한 표현〉

(내 수첩에 당신 이름을 써 주시겠습니까?)

My mother would often tell me folk stories. 〈과거의 불규칙적인 습관〉

(어머니께서는 이따금 내게 옛날 이야기를 들려 주시곤 했다.)

My mother used to tell me folk stories. 〈과거의 규칙적인 습관〉

(어머니께서는 늘 내게 옛날 이야기를 드려 주시곤 했다.)

She used to beat down the price. 〈늘 ~하곤 했다〉

(그녀는 늘 값을 깎곤 했다.)

She was used to beating down the price. 〈~하는 데 익숙하다〉

(그녀는 값을 깎는 데 익숙해 있다.)

There used to be a hotel there. 〈과거의 계속적인 상태〉

(전에 그곳에는 호텔이 있었다.)

We used to live near the station in those days. 〈과거의 계속적인 상태〉

(우리는 그 당시 역 근처에 살았다.)

[주의] 과거의 계속적인 상태를 나타낼 때에는 「used to + 상태동사」의 형식을 취한다.

(4) 「may, might」

일반적으로 조동사의 부정은 조동사 뒤에 부정어 not를 놓아서 부정시키는 것이 원칙이지만 may는 그 뜻에 따라 달리 취급된다. 즉, 허가의 부정은 「must not」으로 "금지"를 나타내고 「may not」은 "약한 금지", 「can not」은 회화체에서

"부드러운 금지"를 나타낸다. 그리고 추측을 나타내는 「may」의 과거형은 「may have + p·p」로 "~이었을지도 모른다"가 된다.

① 일반적인 용법

·May I smoke here? 〈허락, 허가〉

Yes, you may. 〈긍정〉

No, you must not. 〈강한 금지〉

No, you may not. 〈약한 금지〉

No, you can not. 〈회화체에서 사용〉

·The news may be true. 〈추측〉

(= Perhaps the news is true.)

(그 소식은 아마 사실일지도 모른다.)

·The rumor may not be true. 〈추측의 부정〉

(= Perhaps the rumor is not true.)

·She may have been a beauty. 〈과거사실의 추측〉

(=Perhaps she was a beauty.)

(그녀는 아마 옛날에 미인이었을지도 모른다.)

·Though he may be a good student, he is not a good teacher.

〈양보부사절 속에 사용〉

(그가 훌륭한 학생일지는 몰라도 훌륭한 선생은 못된다.)

·He worked hard so that he might live in comfort. 〈목적부사절 속에 사용〉

(그는 안락하게 살기 위해 열심히 일했다.)

·Save money while you may.(= can) 〈가능〉

(가능할 때 저축하라.)

·May God help us! 〈기원〉

(주여, 우리를 도와주소서!)

② 관용적인 표현

·She may well despise you. 〈~하는 것도 당연하다〉

(그녀가 너를 경멸하는 것도 당연하다.)

·You may as well chew your food well. 〈~하는 편이 낫다〉

(음식물은 잘 씹는 편이 낫다.)

·You might as well throw your money into the sea as lend it to him.

〈~하느니 차라리~하는 편이 낫다〉

(네가 그에게 돈을 빌려 주느니 차라리 바다에 던져 버리는 것이 낫다.)

(5) 「must」

이 조동사도 앞에서의 may처럼 부정시키는 방법에 있어서, 의무의 뜻으로 쓰일 때 그것의 부정은 「need not(= don't have to, (英) have not to)」이고, 추측의 뜻으로 쓰일 때 그것의 부정은 「can not」으로 하며, 그것의 과거형은 「must have + p·p」로 한다.

·You must go home before dark. 〈필요, 의무〉

(=You have to go home before dark.)

(어둡기 전에 집으로 가야 한다.)

·Must I go after all? 〈필요, 의무〉

(결국 제가 가야만 합니까?)

→ Yes, you must. 〈긍정〉 / No, you need not. 〈부정〉

(그래, 가야만 합니다. / 아니오, 갈 필요가 없습니다.)

·She looks pale. She must be ill. 〈단정적인 추측〉

(그녀는 얼굴이 창백해 보인다. 그래서 아픈 것임에 틀림없다.)

·I think they must be twins, but she says they cannot be so.

〈단정적 추측 또는 그것의 부정〉

(나는 그들이 쌍둥이임에 틀림없다고 생각하는데 그녀는 그럴 리가 없다고 한다.)

·She must have missed the last train. 〈과거사실의 추측〉

(그녀는 막차를 놓쳤음에 틀림이 없다.)

·He must always have his own way. 〈강한 주장〉

(그는 언제나 자기 멋대로 하려고만 한다.)

·You have only to sit dumb. 〈~하기만 하면 된다.〉

(너는 잠자코 앉아 있기만 하면 된다.)

(6) 「can, could」

① 일반적인 용법

·A bird can fly with its wings. 〈가능, 능력〉

(새라는 동물은 날개로 날 수 있다.)

·I could solve the problem. 〈과거형〉

(나는 그 문제를 풀 수 있었다.)

·I cannot speak Chinese. 〈현재의 부정〉

(나는 중국말을 할 수 없다.)

·I couldn't come here. 〈과거의 부정〉

(나는 이곳에 올 수 없었다.)

·Can I ask you a question? 〈허가〉

(= May I ask you a question?)

(당신에게 질문을 해도 되겠습니까?)

·Can the rumor be true? 〈강한 의심 - 의문문에서〉

(그 소문이 사실일까?)

·Can the rumor have been true? 〈과거사실의 강한 의심〉

(그 소문이 사실이었을까?)

·The report cannot be true. 〈현재의 강한 부정을 추측〉

(그 보도는 사실일 리가 없다.)

·She can be very rude sometimes.

〈현재의 강한 긍정의 추측: ~이 있을 수 있다, ~할 적이 있다.〉

(때때로 그는 대단히 무례한 짓을 할 적이 있다.)

·The report cannot have been true. 〈과거의 강한 부정의 추측〉

(그 보도는 사실이었을 리가 없다.)

·Could you speak more slowly? 〈can보다 공손한 표현〉

(좀더 천천히 말씀해 주시겠습니까?)

(7) 「need, dare, ought (to)」

need와 dare는 의문문·부정문에서 조동사로 주로 사용되고 긍정문에서는 그 뒤에 to 부정사를 취해서 본동사로 사용된다. 물론 본동사로도 부정문·의문문에 사용되기도 한다. 또한 ought는 그 뒤에 to 부정사가 수반되어 사용되는데 그것의 부정은 "ought not to"이다.

① need의 용법

·Need we start so early tomorrow? 〈조동사〉

(내일 그렇게 일찍 출발할 필요가 있습니까?〉

·You need not take the medicine. 〈조동사〉

(너는 그 약을 먹을 필요가 없다.)

·She needs to make a speech. 〈본동사〉

(그녀는 연설할 필요가 있다.)

·She need not give up the plan. 〈조동사〉

(= She does not need to give up the plan.) 〈본동사〉

(그녀는 그 계획을 단념할 필요가 없다.)

·Did you need anything to write with? 〈본동사〉

(필기도구가 필요했습니까?)

·You will need a lot of money to buy it. 〈본동사〉

(네가 그것을 사는 데는 많은 돈이 필요하게 될 것이다.)

·She need not have kept silent. 〈과거의 유감 표시〉

(그녀는 침묵할 필요가 없었는데 했다.)

② dare의 용법

·Dare you jump from the branch? 〈조동사〉

(과감히 나뭇가지로부터 점프하겠니?)

·He dare not go there alone. 〈조동사〉

(그는 감히 혼자서 그곳에 가지 못한다.)

·He dared to speak to the foreigner. 〈본동사〉

(그는 과감히 외국인에게 말을 걸었다.)

·He dares to go out alone after dark. 〈본동사〉

(그는 겁내지 않고 어두워진 후에도 혼자 외출했다.)

③ ought(to)의 용법

·You ought to(= should) help your mother. 〈의무, 당연〉

(너는 어머니를 도와주어야만 한다.)

·We ought not to(= should not) make a noise in the library. 〈의무, 당연의 부정〉

(우리는 도서관 내에서는 떠들지 않아야 한다.)

·She ought to have consulted a doctor. 〈과거의 유감 표시〉

(그녀는 의사에게 진찰을 받았어야 했는데 안 받았다.)

·He ought to arrive here by noon. 〈확정적인 추측〉
(그는 정오까지 이곳에 틀림없이 도착할 것이다.)

C 조동사 활용 문장 익히기 Basic Sentence Drill

맞는 조동사 써 넣기

1. Hi, I don't think I ________ come to work this morning. I'm not sure but I think I have pneumonia.

2. I'm sorry to hear that. ________ you going see your doctor?

3. I'm not sure of it. Probably I ________ .

4. The Bible says, ask and it ________ be given unto you. Also the giving persons are more blessed than who receives.

5. There was no sign of permission to get in. So ________ I to ask " ________ I come in?"And the officer replied so stern that I ________ not.

6. When I was young I ________ to go to church every Sunday but not anymore.

D 응용 영작 Advanced Composition

Level 1

① 그녀는 비행기를 놓친 것임에 *틀림없다.

:

② 그 사람은 20분 안에 도착할 것이다.

:

Level 2

① 당신이 외국인이라면 김치 먹는 데 익숙하지 않을지도 모릅니다.

:

② 그 사람은 *힌두교도이기 때문에 햄버거를 먹을 수 없습니다.

:

Level 3

① 한국인들은 서양문화를 *무비판적으로 *수용해 왔을 것입니다.

:

② * 적자생존원칙은 강자가 약자를 지배한다는 원리일 수도 있습니다.

:

▶ Word Tips for composition

* ~인 것임에 틀림없다: might have + p·p, should have + p·p
* 힌두교도: Hindu
* 무비판적으로: uncritically
* 수용하다: accept
* 적자생존: the Survival of the Fittest

E 응용 독해문 Applied Passages

"Shall I swear by the book which says, 'Swear not at all'?"

Because the Bible says all men are equal in the eyes of God, the Quakers refused to bow to the mighty.

Fox would not take off his hat before kings and judges, and when asked where he could find a Bible text for this, answered, "Shadrach, Meshach, and Abednego went into the fiery furnace with their hose and their coats and their hats on."

F 관련 성경 표현 Related Expression in the Bible

① Matthew 21:22(마태복음 21:22)

If you believe, you will receive whatever you ask for in prayer.

(너희가 기도할 때에 무엇이든지 믿고 구하는 것은 다 받으리라.)

② John 12:36(요한복음 12:36)

*Put your trust in the light while you have it, *so that you may become sons of light.

(너희에게 아직 빛이 있을 동안에 빛을 믿으라. 그리하면 빛의 아들이 되리라.)

* put your trust: 믿으라

* so that ~ may: ~하면 ~할 수 있으리라

③ John 12:37(요한복음 12:37)

Even after Jesus had done all these miraculous signs *in their presence, they still would not *believe in him.

(예수가 이렇게 많은 표적을 저희 앞에서 행하셨으나 저를 믿지 아니하니)

* in their presence: 그들 앞에서(그들이 있는 데서)

* believe in: 믿다

④ Acts 5:29(사도행전 5:29)

Peter and the other apostles replied: We must obey God rather than men!

(베드로와 사도들이 대답하여 가로되 사람보다 하나님을 순종하는 것이 마땅하니라.)

⑤ II Corintians 5:21(고린도후서 5:21)

God made him who had no sin to be sin for us, *so that in him we might become the righteousness of God.

(하나님이 죄를 알지도 못하신 자로 우리를 대신하여 죄를 삼으신 것은 우리로 하여금 저희 안에서 하나님의 의가 되게 하심이니라.)

* so that ~ might: ~해서 ~할 수 있도록.

Free Talking Assignment

여러 가지 조동사를 나열해 보고 각 조동사 활용 예문을 작성해 오자(Q/A).

① can / I can speak English as fluent as my own native language but I can't speak German at all.

② should /

③

④

⑤

⑥

⑦

⑧

⑨

⑩

CHAPTER IV

여러 가지 전치사 이용 말하기

Lesson 10 After arresting him, he put him in prison, handing him over to be guarded by four squads of four soldiers each.

여러 가지 전치사(Prepositions) 이용

A 성경 독해 NIV Reading

Acts 12:4-6

4 After arresting him, he put him in prison, handing him over to
be guarded by four squads of four soldiers each. Herod intended
to bring him out for public trial after the Passover.

5 So Peter was kept in prison, but the church was earnestly
praying to God for him.

6 The night before Herod was to bring him trial, Peter was
sleeping between two soldiers, bound with two chains, and
sentries stood guard at the entrance.

한글성경 참조

사도행전 12:4-6

4 잡으매 옥에 가두어 군인 넷씩인 네 패에게 맡겨 지키고 유월절 후에 백성 앞에 끌어
내고자 하더라

5 이에 베드로는 옥에 갇혔고 교회는 그를 위하여 간절히 하나님께 기도하더라

6 헤롯이 잡아 내려고 하는 그 전날 밤에 베드로가 두 군인 틈에서 두 쇠사슬에 매여 누
워 자는데 파수꾼들이 문 밖에서 옥을 지키더니

B 관련 문법 Related Grammar Review

전치사(preposition)란 명사, 대명사 또는 그 상당어구 앞에서 다른 부분과의 관계를 맺어주는 역할을 하여 내용상으로 다음 같은 여러 가지 종류가 있다.

(1) 「시간 (때)을 나타내는 전치사」

① 「at, in, on」

at - 짧은 시간 표시(시각·정오·일출·일몰)
in - at 보다 긴 시간 표시(월·해·계절·세기), 일반적인 오전·오후·저녁
on - 특정한 날의 시간(오전·오후·저녁), 날짜, 요일

·The train left Seoul at seven.

(기차가 7시에 서울을 출발했다.)

·America declared its independence in 1776.

(미국은 1776년에 독립을 선언했다.)

·People go to the church on Sundays.

(사람들은 일요일마다 교회에 간다.)

② 「in, within, after」

in - 때의 경과 "~이 지나서, ~후에"(현재기준)

within - 일정기간 기준 "~이내에, ~안에"

after - 때의 경과 "~후에"(과거기준)

·He will return in a few days.

(그는 며칠이 지나면 돌아올 것이다.)

·She will be back within a week.

(그녀는 일주일 이내로 돌아올 것이다.)

·He came back after a month.

(그는 한 달이 지나서야 돌아왔다.)

*He will be free after (in) two o'clock.

(그는 2시 정각이 지나서 풀려나게 될 것이다.)

③ 「by, till, until」

by - (동작의 완료): "~까지"

till - (동작·상태의 계속): "~까지"

until - till 보다 다소 강조적, 주문 앞에 선행절을 이끌 때 주로 사용

·I shall be back by six.

(6시까지는 돌아오겠다.)

·I waited for him until(till) three.

(나는 3시까지 그를 기다리겠다.)

·Stay here until(till) the end of next month.

(다음날 말까지 이곳에서 머물러라.)

④ 「for, during, through」

for - (일정하고 구체적인 기간, 주로 수사 동반): "~동안에"

during - (특정 사건·기간 앞에 사용): "~동안에, ~중에"

throught - (일정 시간의 처음부터 끝까지 계속): "~줄곧, 내내"

·I haven't seen her for three days.

(나는 그녀를 3일 동안 보지 못했다.)

·He was asleep during the lesson.

(그는 수업 중에 졸았다.)

·I stayed in Swiss through the vacation.

(나는 방학 내내 스위스에서 머물렀다.)

⑤ 「since, from」

since - (과거의 어느 시점부터 현재까지 계속): "~이래로 죽"

from - (일정 시점의 출발점만 표시, 현재까지 계속은 아님): "~부터"

[주의] 「- hood」형 추상명사와 함께 쓰일 때는 현재까지의 계속일지라도 "from"을 사용하고, 또한 「시작」의 의미를 가진 동사들 "begin, start, commence"와 함께 쓸 때에는 시간의 기점으로 "from"을 사용하지 않는다.

·I have not heard from him since last month.

(나는 지난달부터 줄곧 그에 대한 소식을 듣지 못하고 있다.)

·I lived in Seoul from 1979 to 1993.

(나는 1979년부터 1993년까지 서울에 살았다.)

·I have Known him from his childhood.

(나는 그와 어린시절부터 줄곧 알고 지내 오는 사이이다.)

·School begins at nine.

(수업은 9시에 시작한다.)

(2) 장소를 나타내는 전치사

① 「on, beneath」

on - (어떤 표면의 접착 상태에서): "~위에"

beneath - (어떤 표면의 접착 상태에서): "~아래에"

·There is a church on the hill.

(언덕 위에 교회가 있다.)

·There is a coin beneath the pillow.

(베게 밑에 동전 하나가 있다.)

② 「at, in」

at - (비교적 좁은 장소) 집, 거리, 마을: "~에"

in - (비교적 넓은 장소, 내부) 도시, 나라: "~에, ~안에"

·She is now staying at the village.

(그녀는 지금 그 마을에 머무르고 있다.)

·He found a position in Seoul.

(그는 서울에서 일자리를 얻었다.)

·He lives in this village. 〈자기가 살고 있는 곳은 "in"〉

(그는 이 마을에서 살고 있다.)

·On my last trip I stopped at Chicago. 〈잠깐 거쳐가는 곳은 "at"〉

(지난번 여행에서 나는 시카고에 잠깐 들렀다.)

③ 「over, under, above, below」

over - (일정한 거리를 유지한 상태): "~위에"
under - (일정한 거리를 유지한 상태): "~아래"
above - (막연한 거리, 비스듬한 상태): "~보다 높이에"
below - (막연한 거리, 비스듬한 상태): "~보다 아래에"

·There is a long bridge over the river.

(강 위에 긴 다리가 있습니다.)

·There is a cat under the table.

(탁자 밑에 고양이가 있습니다.)

·The birds flew above the trees.

(새들이 나무 위로 날아다녔다.)

·The moon sank below the horizon.

(수평선 아래로 달이 졌다.)

④ 「up, down」

up - (운동 동반): "~ 위로"
down - (운동 동반): "~ 아래로"

·He was climbing up the mountain.

(그는 산 위로 올라가고 있었다.)

·He was running down the stairs.

(그는 계단 아래로 달려 내려갔다.)

⑤ 「before, after, behind」

before - (정지상태에서): "~앞에"

after - (운동상태에서): "~뒤에, ~뒤를 쫓아"

behind - (정지 또는 운동상태에서): "~뒤에"

·You must stand before me. 〈생물과 함께 쓰인다.〉

(내 앞에 꼼짝 말고 서 있어야 한다.)

·The dog was running after the cat.

(그 개는 고양이의 뒤를 쫓아갔다.)

·He was hiding behind a door.

(그는 현관문 뒤에 숨어 있었다.)

·I will meet you in front of the library tomorrow. 〈무생물과 함께 쓰인다.〉

(내일 도서관 앞에서 만납시다.)

·Shut the door after you.

(들어오고 문 닫아라.)

·Shut the door behind you.

(네 뒤의 문을 닫아라.)

⑥ 「by, beside, at」

by, beside - (우연한 접근): "~옆에"

at - (의식적인 접근): "~옆에"

·There is a pine tree by the well.

(우물 옆에 소나무가 있다.)

·Someone is at the door.

(어떤 사람이 현관문에 있다.)

·Come and sit beside me.

(와서 내 옆에 앉아라.)

·There is a park beside our school.

(우리 학교 옆에 공원이 있습니다.)

A Letter from Seoul 125

⑦「between, among」

betweem - (둘 사이에서): "~사이에"

among - (셋 이상 사이에서): "~사이에"

[주의] amidst (다른 종류의 사이)

among (같은 종류의 사이)

·I sat down between the two ladies.

(나는 두 숙녀 사이에 앉았다.)

·Birds are singing among the trees.

(새들이 나무 사이에서 노래 부르고 있다.)

·He was found among the dead. (그는 죽었다.)

·He was found amidst the dead. (그는 살았다.)

⑧ 「along, across, through」

along - (처음과 끝의 한계가 명확하지 않은 곳을 지나는 경우): "~을 따라서"
across - (처음과 끝의 한계가 명확한 곳을 지나는 경우): "~을 횡단하여"
through - (어느 곳을 완전히 관통하여 지나가는 경우): "~을 지나서, ~관통하여"

·The trees are planted along the street.
(나무들이 거리를 따라(길게) 심어져 있다.)
·Take care when you go across the street.
(거리를 횡단할 때 조심하십시오.)
·The river flows through the city.
(강물이 도시를 관통해서 흐르고 있다.)

⑨ 「around, round, about」

around - (정지상태): "주위에, 주위를 둘러싼"
round - (운동상태): "주위에, 주위를 도는"
about - (막연한 주위): "여기저기에"

·We sat around the fire.
(우리는 모닥불 주위를 둘러싸고 앉았다.)
·The moon goes round(=around) the earth.
(달은 지구 주위를 돌고 있다.)
·I walked about the town.
(나는 마을 여기저기를 걸어 다녔다.)

⑩ 「to, for, toward(s), from」

to - (방향과 도착지점): "~으로, ~에"
for - (분명한 목적지와 방향): "~을 향하여"
toward(s) - (불분명한 목적지로써 운동의 방향만 표시): "~쪽으로"
from - (출발지점): "~으로부터"

·She went to Paris to study art.
(그녀는 미술을 공부하러 파리로 갔다.)
·He has left Seoul for Pusan.
(그는 부산을 향하여 서울을 떠났다.)
·He was running towards the North.
(그는 북쪽으로 달려갔다.)
·He started from Seoul.
(그는 서울에서 출발했다.)

⑪ 「into, out of, in」

into - (내부로 들어가는 운동 방향): "~안으로"
out of - (외부로 나가는 운동 방향): "~밖으로"
in - (내부의 정지상태): "~안에"

·He went into the room and out of it again.
(그는 방 안으로 들어왔다가 다시 밖으로 나왔다.)
·There are two birds in the cage.
(새장 안에 두 마리의 새가 있습니다.)

(3) 원인·이유를 나타내는 전치사

① 「from, of, through」

from - (사망과 질병의 간접적 원인): "~으로, ~때문에"

of - (사망과 질병의 직접적 원인): "~으로, ~때문에"

through - (소극적, 중개적 원인): "~으로, ~때문에"

·He was taken ill from eating too much.

(그는 과식으로 인해 병이 들었다.)

·He died of Cholera.

(그는 콜레라로 죽었다.)

·He lost his position through his idleness.

(그는 근무 태만으로 직업을 잃었다.)

② 「for, with」

for - (마음에 대한 무형의 원인): "~으로, 때문에"

with - (외부에서 육체에 미치는 원인): "~으로, 때문에"

·I couldn't speak for fear.

(나는 두려움 때문에 말할 수 없었다.)

·She was shivering with cold.

(그녀는 추위 때문에 몸을 떨었다.)

③ 「on, at, in, over」

on - (동작이나 행위의 결과): "~으로, 때문에"
at - (감정의 원인): "~보고, 듣고"
in - (기쁨, 자부심의 원인 또는 동기): "~으로, 때문에"
over - (감정의 원인): "~에 대하여, ~으로"

·I congratulate you on your success.
(당신의 성공을 축하 드립니다.)

·I am surprised at his coming to see me.
(그가 나를 만나러 온다는 소식을 듣고 나는 놀랐다.)

·She takes delight in music lessons.
(그녀는 음악 수업으로 인해 즐거웠다.)

·He mourned over her sudden death.
(그는 그녀의 갑작스런 죽음에 대하여 슬퍼했다.)

(4) 목적을 나타내는 전치사

for - (목적, 추구, 준비): "~하기 위해서"
on - (용무, 여행, 목적): "~하러, ~차, ~로"
after - (추구, 욕망): "~을 구하고자"

·Many Koreans go abroad for study.
(많은 한국인들은 연구 목적으로 외국으로 나간다.)

·He went to Seoul on business.
(그는 사업상으로 서울로 갔다.)

·He is always seeking after wealth.
(그는 언제나 부〈富〉를 추구하고 있다.)

(5) 원료·재료를 나타내는 전치사

of - (재료를 나타내며 물리적 변화): "~ 상태에서, ~위에"
form - (원료를 나타내며 화학적 변화): "~으로"
into - (원료가 제품화 되는 것): "~으로"

·This house is made of stone. 〈=out of〉
(이 집은 돌로 만들어졌다.)
·Wine is made from grapes.
(포도주는 포도로 만들어졌다.)
·Milk is made into butter.
(우유는 가공이 되어 버터가 된다.)

(6) 수단, 방법, 행위자 표시를 나타내는 전치사

by - (행위자 및 수단 표시): "~에 의해서, ~으로"
with - (도구표시): "~으로"
through - (중개, 경로를 표시): "~을 통해서"

·He was killed by a robber.
(그는 강도에 의해 살해당했다.)
·He was killed with a pistol.
(그는 권총으로 살해당했다.)
·He spoke to him through an interpreter.
(그는 통역관을 통해 그에게 말했다.)

(7) 결과를 나타내는 전치사

to - (동작의 결과): "~해서, ~으로"
into - (변화의 결과): "~으로"

·She cried herself to sleep.
(그녀는 울다가 잠들었다.)
·The beggar was frozen to death.
(거지는 얼어서 죽었다.)
·Water changes into ice when cooled.
(물은 차가와지면 얼음으로 변한다.)

(8) 계량, 비교, 교환을 나타내는 전치사

by - (계량의 단위): "~으로, ~당"
for - (비교, 교환): "~에 비해서"
to(with): "~에 비하여, ~에, ~로"

·They sell sugar by the pound.
(파운드로 설탕을 팔고 있다.)
·I bought the book for 3,000Won.
(나는 그 책을 3,000원 주고 구입했다.)
·We often compare life to a comedy.
(우리는 자주 인생을 하나의 희극에 비유한다.)
·Compare this with that.
(이것을 저것과 비교해 봐라.)

(9) 그 밖의 전치사

of - (인물, 사물의 존재): "~에 관하여"
about - (상세한 사정): "~에 관하여"
on - (연구, 논문의 주제): "~에 관하여"
with - (관련, 관계): "~과"
after - (모방, 흉내): "~을 본떠서"

C 기본 문장 익히기 Basic Sentence Drill

맞는 전치사 써 넣기

Please fill in the blanks with proper preposition.

1. Washington D.C. is the capital city ________ the U.S.A.
2. Mrs. Kim is very submissive ________ her husband so she always does what he asks ________ her to do.
3. ________ this little amount ________ money, we can't buy many things we need.
4. How far is it ________ Pusan ________ Seoul?
5. Marine biologists are people who have their researches ________ the living things ________ the sea.

6. What are you talking ________? I can't understand the whole story.

7. Everybody is laughing ________ him ________ he always says nonsense.

8. The subject I am most interested ________ is Biblical archeology.

9. Please wake me up exactly ________ six o'clock ________ the morning.

10. I was born ________ 1976. The exact time of my birth is not very accurate. I just remember my mother saying it was ________ the evening ________ one rainy day. But my aunt says it ________ was noon and my uncle says it was the middle ________ the night.

11. They say, there is happiness ________ the rainbow and I think that means we have to look ________ reality.

12. Please sit ________ me, so that I can hold your hand.

13. This pretty doll is made ________ cloth and beer is brewed ________ barley.

14. As in Korea, the proverb "catching two birds ________ one stone" is commonly used and is supposed to mean having a double-effect with a certain amount ________ effort.

15. My grandmother was suffering lung ________ cancer ________ a long time and she eventually died ________ that disease.

16. I drove ________ the beautiful tree-arched paths ________ the sidewalk.

D 응용 영작 Advanced Composition

Level 1

① 그는 한국에서 1949년에 태어났다.

:

② 배는 *해안을 따라서 *항해했다.

:

Level 2

① 다리 저편에 무지개가 있습니다.

:

② 그 *예배에 *참석할 수 없어서 *유감입니다.

:

Level 3

① 그러한 악조건하에서(나쁜 환경에서) 그는 결국 성공했다.

:

② 신세대와 구세대 사이에는 심각한 문화적 차이가 존재합니다.

:

▸ **Word Tips for composition**

* 해안: sea-coast
* 항해하다: sail, cruise, launch
* 예배: chapel, service, worship
* 참석하다: participate in, take part in
* 유감이다: be regretful, be sorry for~

E 응용 독해문 Applied Passages

He was again laid aside by sickness, and appeared to be dying.

His anxieties and fears returned, and he was sinking into despair.

An old monk entered his cell, and spoke kindly to him.

Luther told him of his misery and fear.

The old man could not counsel like Staupitz, but he knew his creed, and it had comforted his heart.

Simply he repeated, “I believe in the forgiveness of sins.”

The sick man slowly said the words, “I believe in the forgiveness of sins.”

“Ah!” exclaimed the aged brother, “you must believe not only in the forgiveness of David's and Peter's sins, but you must believe that your own sins are forgiven.”

F 관련 성경 표현 Related Expression in the Bible

① Revelation 13:1(요한계시록 13:1)

And I saw a beast coming out of the sea. He had ten horns and seven heads, with then crowns on his horns, and on each head a *blasphemous name.

(내가 보니 바다에서 한 짐승이 나오는데 뿔이 열이요 머리가 일곱이라. 그 뿔에는 열 면류관이 있고 그 머리들에는 참람된 이름들이 있더라.)

* blasphemous: 참람된, 신성모독의 ⓝblasphemy

② Psalms 23:2(시편 23:2)

He makes me lie down in green pastures he leads me beside quiet waters.

(그가 나를 푸른 초장에 누이시며 쉴만한 물가로 인도하시는도다.)

③ Psalms 23:4(시편 23:4)

Even though I walk through the valley of the shadow of death, I will fear no evil, for you are with me.

(내가 사망의 음침한 골짜기로 다닐지라도 해를 두려워하지 않을 것은 주께서 나와 함께 하심이라.)

④ Psalms 23:5(시편 23:5)

You prepare a table before me in the presence of my enemies. You *anoint my head with oil; my cup overflows.

(주께서 내 원수의 목전에서 내게 상을 베푸시고 기름으로 내 머리에 바르셨으니 내 잔이 넘치나이다.)

* anoint one's head: 기름으로 머리를 바르다, 안수하다

⑤ Isaiah 39:17(이사야 39:17)

Surely it was for my benefit that I suffered such anguish. In your love you kept me from *the pit of destruction. You have put all my sins behind your back.

(보옵소서 내게 큰 고통을 더 하신 것은 내게 평안을 주려 하심이라. 주께서 나의 영혼을 사랑하사 멸망의 구덩이에서 건지셨고 나의 모든 죄는 주의 등 뒤에 던지셨나이다.)

* the pit of destruction: 멸망의 구덩이

전치사의 숙어적인 용법인 구 전치사(Phrase Preposition)

◎ 구 전치사(Phrase Preposition)

두 개 이상의 말이 모여서 하나의 전치사 구실을 하는 것인데, 구전치사(Group Preposition), 또는 전치사구(Preposition Phrase)라고도 한다. 이것은 숙어로서 외워야 할 것이며, 그 수도 많아 여기에 다 들 수 없다.

1. as to = about「…에 관해서」
2. instead of「…대신에」
3. on account of「… 때문에」

   Thoughts are expressed by means of words.(사상은 말에 의해 표현된다.)

   He succeeded in spite of all difficulties.(온갖 곤란에도 불구하고 그는 성공했다.)
4. according to: ~에 따라서, ~에 의하면
5. honour of: ~을 위하여, ~ 때문에
6. in consequence of: ~때문에, ~의 결과로

   due to + 명사(형용사구): ~때문에

due to + 동·원: ~예정인

because of + 명사(부사구): ~때문에

7. for the sake(good, benefit) of: ~을 위하여

8. for the purpose of

with a view of ~을 할 목적으로

with the object of

9. for want of: ~이 결핍하여 〈부사구〉

in want of: ~이 결핍한 〈형용사구〉

10. by way of: ~을 경유하여

by means of: ~의 수단으로, ~의 힘으로

by dint of: ~의 덕택으로, ~힘으로

11. instead of: ~대신에, ~하지 않고

12. in addition to: ~에 첨가하여

13. as to: ~에 관하여 as for: ~에 관한 한

14. in behalf of: ~을 위하여

on behalf of: ~을 대신하여, ~대리로서

15. in case of: ~을 위하여

in search of: ~을 찾아서

in front of: ~앞에

in spite of: ~에도 불구하고

in favour of: ~에 찬성하여, ~을 위해

in pursuit of: ~을 추구하여

선교
영어
회화

English For Mission

CHAPTER V

가산·
불가산 명사
이용 말하기

Lesson 11

Take this ephah of roasted grain and these ten loves of bread for your brothers.

가산(可算) 명사와 불가산(不可算) 명사의 종류;

불가산 명사의 가산화(可算化)

A 독해 Reading

There is some ice cream and some yogurt in my refregerator. My friend Linda and I are going to have a scoop of ice cream for dessert after we finish our supper.

Also we have a few of apples, two dozens of eggs and several tomatoes.

A quart of milk is for our breakfast to go with several pieces of toasts.

My family loves to eat continental breakfast almost every morning.

So I'd better prepare a pack of bacon, too.

For lunch, we are going to make pizza but unfortunately, we don't have any cheese left.

Even worse,

I do not keep the recipe and don't know exactly how to cook.

Besides that, my sister goes on diet and she has to reduce a certain amount of calories.

Probably, onions, beans, and many different kinds of vegetables are recommendable for her, everyday.

▸▸ Questions

1. What did you have for breakfast?

2. What will you have for your lunch?

3. What are you going to eat for your supper?

4. Please tell me your three favorite dishes and talk about the materials used.

① ______________________________

② ______________________________

③ ______________________________

5. Can you classify the kind of Nouns as below?

Count Nouns	Non-Count Nouns
tomato(tomatoes) apple(apples)	ice cream bread

B 관련 문법 Related Grammar Review

명사를 형태상으로 분류하면 「셀 수 있는 명사(가산명사)와 셀 수 없는 명사(불가산명사)」의 두 가지로 나눌 수 있고, 의미상으로 분류하면 「보통명사·집합명사·고유명사·추상명사·물질명사」의 다섯 가지로 나눌 수 있다.

집합명사 중에는 셀 수 없는 명사에 속하는 것도 있다(furniture, produce…).

형태상 분류	의미상 분류	변형
셀 수 있는 명사(가산명사)	보통명사	the + 보통명사 = 추상명사
	집합명사	(*군집명사)
셀 수 없는 명사(불가산명사)	추상명사	보통명사화
	물질명사	보통명사화
	고유명사	보통명사화

셀 수 있는 명사란 사람·동물·식물 따위 이외에 제품·행위 등의 구체적인 것들을 말하며, 그것에 비해 셀 수 없는 명사란 물질이나 관념 따위를 나타내는 것을 말한다. 그러나 셀 수 없는 명사로 분류된 것들이 반드시 그것으로만 쓰이는 것이 아니라 때로는 문장 속에서 셀 수 있는 명사로 변형되는 경우도 있는데, 이때 뜻의 변화도 수반되기 때문에 주의해야 된다.

She is a beauty of our age. 〈보통명사화: 미인〉
(그녀는 당대의 미인이다.)
Beauty is but skin-deep. 〈추상명사: 아름다움, 미(美)〉
(아름다움(미모)도 따지고 보면 가죽 한 꺼풀. - 즉, 얼굴이 예쁘다고 마음마저 예쁘다는 법은 없다.)

그러면 셀 수 있는 명사와 셀 수 없는 명사의 사용 시에 있어서 차이점을 살펴보면 다음과 같다.

셀 수 있는 명사(가산명사)	셀 수 없는 명사(불가산명사)
① 명사 앞에 "a(n), the, this, that, no, any, some"이나 「수」를 나타내는 many가 붙는다.	① 명사 앞에 "a(n), the, this, that, no, any, some"을 붙일 수 없으며, 「양」을 나타내는 much를 쓸 수 있다.
② 단수·복수 모두가 가능하다 단수형만 가능하다	단수형만 가능하다.

※ 그러나, 명사 앞에 그 명사를 세는 계량명사를 써서 가산명사화할 수 있다.

※ 여러 가지 불가산명사 앞에 적합한 계량명사를 사용하여 가산화할 수 잇는 실례를 들어보자. 그리고 그 표현을 외워 버리자!

1. 음식물의 경우

·a cup of coffee → (many cups of coffee)

·a glase of milk →

·a bottle of orange juice →

·a bowl of vegetable soup →

·a piece of bread →

a (slice) of bread →

a (lump) of bread →

a (loaf) of bread →

·a head of lettuce →

·an ear of corn →

·a pound of sugar(salt, pepper, flour, rice 등) →

·a bar(stick) of cheese →

·a jar of jam →

·a scoop of ice cream →

·a cluster of grape →

·an order of pancake(scrambled egg) →

·a spoonful of garlic powder(sugar, salt, flour etc.) →

등등 각 음식종류별로 거의 다 가산화할 수 있다.

2. 동물·짐승의 떼 또는 사람의 떼

·a herd of cattle

·a flock of sheep

·a swarm of bees

·a yoke of oxen

·a brace of hare

·a school of fish

·a covey of quail

·a multitude of people

·a host of people etc.

3. 추상명사의 복수화

·a piece of advice (충고 한마디)

·an act of kindness (한 번의 친절한 행동)

·a bit of scandal (한 번의 추문)

·a series of misfortune (일련의 불행한 사건)

·a strike of grief (한 바탕치고 간 슬픔) etc.

4. 자연현상을 구체적인 수량형용사구를 붙여쓸 때에도

·a flash.(flash.) of lightening (한 차례의 번개)

·a strike of thunder (한 차례의 천둥)

·a shower of rain (한 차례의 비)

·a roar(shout) of laughter (한바탕의 웃음)

·a bit of nonsense (한마디 허튼소리)

·a case of theft (한 건의 절도)

·a third of income (수입의 1/3) etc.

C 관련문형 익히기 Basic Sentence Drill

Circle the correct expression.

What's your recipe for making Kimchi, Young Ja? It's not very difficult.

First, put a [little / few of] salt into many [heads / bags] of Chinese cabbages.

After that, few of bags

chop up a [little / few(of)] green onions and a [little / few] garlic. (of)

Then cut some cabbages

and add [many / much] sugar stirred in the water. Prepare [much / many] red pepper to pour in.

Slice some radishes and stir them up with many different kinds of Korean seasonings.

D 응용 영작 Advanced Composition

Level 1

① 우리는 *아침식사로 계란 3개와 1병의 우유 그리고 5쪽의 빵이 필요합니다.

:

② 양상추 3통과 두 판의 팬케익이 *주문 중에 있습니다.

:

Level 2

① 한 번의 친절한 행동이 한바탕의 웃음을 가져다 줍니다.

:

② 한마디의 허튼소리가 일련의 불행한 사건을 가져올 수도 있습니다.

:

Level 3

① 지난주 뉴욕시내에서 많은 절도건수가 있었습니다.

:

② 그 *대학교무과에 전화하면 *입학지원서 외에 많은 정보를 얻을 수 있을 것입니다.

:

▶ Word Tips for composition

* 아침식사로: for breakfast
* 주문 중에 있다: be in order

* 가져다주다: bring
* 대학교무과: the office of Academic Affairs
  (美) Registration Office
* 입학지원서: the Application Form

E 응용 독해문 Applied Passages

I ran out to the landing, and the whole house was full of smoke.

The house was on fire, and it looked like I was alone in it.

I went down the back stairway, which didn't seem so full of smoke, but the door that let out onto the first-floor landing was locked, and I had to go back up again.

By the time I got back up, the front stairway was a great deal fuller of smoke, and I could see glints of flame winking through it way down below.

But it was my only way out of that place.

On the top step I stumbled over a gray wool bunch of something or other, and I picked it up in my mouth. Think I, "That is Freckles's gray sweater, that he is so stuck on.

I might as well take it down to him." It wasn't so hard for a lively dog to get out of a place like that, I thought.

F 관련 성경구절 Related Expression in the Bible

① Genesis 41:27(창세기 41:27)

The seven lean, ugly cows that came up afterward are seven years, and so are *the seven worthless heads of grain *scorched by the east wind. They are seven years of *famine.

(그 후에 올라온 파리하고 흉악한 일곱 소는 칠 년이요 동풍에 말라 속이 빈 일곱 이삭도 일곱 해 흉년이니.)

* the seven worthless heads of grain: 속이 빈 일곱 이삭
* scorched by: ~에 말라 버린, ~타 버린
* famine: 기근, 흉년

② Genesis 45:22(창세기 45:22)

To each of them he gave new clothing, but to Benjamin he gave three hundred shekels of silver and five sets of clothes.

(또 그들에게 다 각기 옷 한 벌씩 주되 베냐민에게는 은 삼백과 옷 다섯 벌을 주고)

③ II Samuel 6:19(사무엘하 6:19)

Then he gave a loaf of bread, a cake of dates and cake of raisins to each person in the whole crowd of Israelites, both men and women.

(모든 백성 곧 온 이스라엘 무리의 무론 남녀하고 떡 한 개와 고기 한 조각과 건포도 떡 한덩이씩 나눠주매.)

④ Song of Songs 4:1(아가서 4:1)

Your hair is like a flock of goats *descending from Mount Gilead.

(네 머리털은 길르앗 산 기슭에 누운 무리 염소 같구나.)

* descending from ~에서 내려온

→ (~기슭에 누운)

⑤ Song of Songs 4:4(아가서 4:4)

Your neck is like the tower of David, built with elegance; on it hang a thousand shields, all of them *shields of warriors.

(네 목은 군기를 두려고 건축한 다윗의 망대 곧 일천방패, 용사의 모든 방패가 달린 망대같고)

* shields of warriors: 용사의 방패

Free talking assignment

1. What is your favorite food and the recipe? Bring the recipe and share.
2. To prepare the materials please make up your shopping list in detail.

CHAPTER VI

형용사의 비교문 이용 말하기

Lesson 12

Greater love has no one than this, that he lay down his life for his friends.

형용사의 비교: 원급, 비교급, 최상급 문장 이용

A 성경 독해 NIV Reading

John 15:9-13

9 “As the Father has loved me, so have I loved you. Now remain in
my love.
10 If you obey my commands, you will remain in my love, just as I
have obeyed my Father's commands and remain in his love.
11 I have told you this so that my joy may be in you and that your
joy may be complete.
12 My command is this: Love each other as I have loved you.
13 Greater love has no one than this, that he lay down his life for
his friends.

한글성경 참조

요한 15:9-13

9 아버지께서 나를 사랑하신 것 같이 나도 너희를 사랑하였으니 나의 사랑 안에 거하라
10 내가 아버지의 계명을 지켜 그의 사랑 안에 거하는 것 같이 너희도 내 계명을 지키면
내 사랑 안에 거하리라
11 내가 이것을 너희에게 이름은 내 기쁨이 너희 안에 있어 너희 기쁨을 충만하게 하려
함이라
12 내 계명은 곧 내가 너희를 사랑한 것 같이 너희도 서로 사랑하라 하는 이것이니라
13 사람이 친구를 위하여 자기 목숨을 버리면 이보다 더 큰 사랑이 없나니

B 관련문법 Related Grammar Review

With a *rapid growth of economic situation, Korea now has been enjoying the *prosperity.

But when I was growing up it was not as good as it is.

People were kind but a great majority of people had severe financial difficulty.

At that time, until about a hundred years ago, *the largest portion of the population, the class had the smallest portion of income.

Besides that, Koreans have more *conservative attitude about money than Americans do.

Now the opposite occurs as general phenomena.

People become less kind and they don't want to be involved in each other as much as they were because they just want to enjoy their own life of having more abundant materials.

They go shopping, eat out with their families so often, etc.

There has been the remarkable change in the field of its transportation.

Public transportation such as bus system, subway, taxi and a various kinds of automobiles can virtually reach anywhere in the country shortly.

The worst thing in the city of Seoul is the traffic jam.

You cannot *make an appointment during the day time *unless you use the public transportation.

Influenced by Christian values, which emphasizes family importance now a days families enjoy more activities together.

They go out and eat together more often.

In the past, the women used to eat at a separate table or after the men ate.

In the thought of *Confucianism men are generally regarded as being *superior to women. It is not anymore like that.

The life, *on the whole, in many areas is much more convenient than the past, but in its spiritual well-being, as many other counturies, it becomes more and more *sterile.

However, Korea has its name value for the strongest Christian church growth in whole Asia.

▸▸ Questions

Please check if the statement made below is true or false. (○ / ×)

1. In recent years Korea seems pretty stable, compare to the past. (   )
2. The more the economic situation develops, the kinder the people of Korea becomes. (   )
3. In the past, farmers were the richest class in the country. (   )
4. Koreans have more conservative thought about money. (   )
5. Among all other areas the public transportation has attained its fastest change. (   )
6. The traffic jam and the stop-and-go situation is not any more a problem in the city of Seoul. (   )
7. Christians are not as family-oriented as Buddhists. (   )
8. In the thought of Confucianism men are definitely inferior to women. (   )
9. Korea is very important in the study of church growth when we consider that it has the most church population in all Asian countries. (   )

B 관련 문법 Related Grammar Review

성질·상태·정도·수량·우월 등을 나타냄에 있어 서로 간의 차이를 나타내기 위해서 형용사 또는 부사의 어형을 바꾸는 것을 비교하고 하는데, 여기에는 다른 것과 비교하지 않고 성질·수량 따위를 나타내는 원급(Positive Degree), 두 개 중에서 한 쪽이 다른 쪽보다 정도가 높은 것을 나타내는 비교급(Comparative Degree), 세 개 중에서 어느 하나가 정도에 있어서 최상의 상태를 나타내는 최상급(Superlative Degree)의 세 가지가 있다. 이러한 비교급과 최상급을 만드는 방법에는 규칙적인 것과 불규칙적인 변화가 있기 때문에 주의해야 한다.

1. 형태

(1) **규칙변화:** 단음절어 전부와 일부의 2음절어는 형용사 또는 부사의 어미에 「-er(비교급), -est(최상급)」를 붙이고, 3음절 형용사 또는 부사는 그 앞에 「more(비교급), most(최상급)」로 수식한다.

① 1음절의 낱말은 원급에 「- er(비교급), - est(최상급)」

tall - taller - tallest

rich - richer - richest

② 2음절어 낱말에서도 어미가 "-er, -le, -y, -ow, -some"로 끝나는 것들과 악센트가 둘째 음절에 있는 것들은 원급에 「-er(비교급), -est(최상급)」, 단 early를 제외하고 "-ly"로 끝나는 부사에는 모두 "more·most"를 붙여 나타낸다.

tender(상냥한) - tenderer- tenderest

noble(고상한) - nobler - noblest

polite(정중한) - politer - politest

profound(심원한) - profounder - profoundest

severe(엄함) - severer - severest

[주의] early(이른, 일찍) - earlier - earliest

kindly(친절히) - more kindly - most kindly

slowly(천천히) - more slowly - most slowly

또한 hostile, docile, fertile, proper, eager 등과 2음절어에서 앞에 악센트가 있는 honest, common, cruel, quiet, pleasant, stupid 등은 그 앞에 more·most를 붙인다.

③ 이 밖의 2음절의 낱말(어미가 -able, -al, -ed, -dul, -ing, -ive, -ant, -ent, -less, -ous…)이나 3음절의 낱말 모두에는 「more(비교급), most(최상급)」

eatable(먹을 수 있는) - more eatable - most eatable

learned(학식있는) - more learned - most learned

loving(사랑하는) - more loving - most loving

foolish(바보스런) - more foolish - most foolish

careless(부주의한) - more careless - most careless

beautiful(아름다운) - more beautiful - most beautiful

interesting(재미있는) - more interesting - most interesting

[주의] 2음절 낱말에서 「-er, -est」를 붙이는 것들은 부정접두사가 붙어 3음절이 되어도 그대로 「-er, -est」를 붙인다.

·impolite - impoliter - impolitest

④ 어미가 「단모음 + 단자음」의 경우에는 끝의 자음을 중복시킨 다음 -er(비교급), -est(최상급)을 만들며, 그리고 어미가 「자음 + y」이면 「자음 + ier, iest」으로 하고 「모음 + y」이면 그대로 어미에 「-er, -est」를 붙인다.

wet - wetter - wettest

pretty - prettier - prettiest

coy - coyer - coyest

⑤ 다음의 경우에는 단음절이나 2음절인 경우인데도 「more, most」를 붙이는 경우이다.

·서술적 용법으로 쓰이는 낱말들

fond, worth, afraid, content, alive, alone, aware …

·습관적으로 쓰이는 낱말들

like, real, just, right, wrong, false, strange …

·동일인·동일물의 두 가지 성질을 비교할 때는 「more ~ than형식」을 취하나 단음절의 단위표시 형용사에서는 동일물의 비교일지라도 「-er than 형식」을 취한다.

He is more clever than wise.

The wall is thicker than (it is) high.

(2) 불규칙 변화(Irregular Comparison)-외워 버리자!

원급	비교급	최상급
good (좋은) well (건강한, 잘)	better	best
bad (나쁜) ill (병든, 나쁘게)	worse	worst
many (수 - 많은) much (양 - 많은)	more	most
old (나이 든, 손위의)	(연령) older (장유, 형제)	elder oldest eldest
far (먼)	(거리) farther (정도) further	farthest furthest
late (늦은)	(시간) later (순서) latter	latest (최근의) last (최후의)
near (가까운)	nearer	(거리) nearest (순서) next
fore (앞의)	former	(거리) foremost (순서) first
little (적은, 작은)	littler (smaller) less	littlest (smallest) least

·My elder brother is older than your eldest sister.
(나의 형) (나이가 많은) (큰누나)

·He lost his only son in his later days.
(만년에)

·I like the latter part of the story.
(후반부)

2. 비교의 여러 형식

(1) 원급비교(동등비교)

둘 사이를 비교해서 그 정도가 같은 것임을 나타내는 비교의 형식이다.

① as + 원급 + as : ~ 만큼 …한

not as (또는 so) + 원급 + as~ : ~ 만큼 …않은

② as + 원급 + as any + 명사

as + 원급 + as ever + 동사 〉어느 ~ 에도 못지않게 〈원급 → 최상급〉

③ as ~ as possible

as ~ as one can 〉가능한 한, 될 수 있는 대로

④ as ~ as can be

as ~ as anything 〉더할 나위없이 ~ 한

⑤ nothing(no + 명사) is so + 원급 + as ~ : ~ 만큼 …한 것은 없다. 〈원급 → 최상급〉

⑥ not so much ~ as … : ~ 이라기 보다는 오히려…

not so much as + 동사 : ~ 조차 않다. (없다.)

(= not even + 동사)

⑦ ~ times as + 원급 + as : 의 ~ 배

⑧ ⓐ as well as ⓑ

not only ⓐ but also ⓑ 〉뿐만 아니라 ~ 도 마찬가지로

·He is as kind as she (is kind). - 형용사

(그는 그녀만큼 친절하다.)

·He is not so (or as) kind as she (is kind). - 열등비교

(그는 그녀만큼 친절하지 못하다.)

·I know her as well as you do. (= you know her) - 부사
(네가 그녀를 알고 있는 만큼 나도 그녀를 잘 알고 있다.)

·Women are as good mechanics as men are good mechanics) nowadays. - 명사
(오늘날에는 여성도 남성만큼이나 기계를 잘 다룬다.)

·He is as wise a man as ever lived.
(= He is the wisest man that ever lived.)
(그는 지금까지 존재해 온 어느 누구 못지않게 현명한 사람이다.)

·Mother is as busy as ever. 〈여전히, 다시 없이〉
(어머니는 여전히 바쁘시다.)

·He is as good a teacher as I ever knew.
(그는 지금까지 내가 알고 지내 온 사람 중에 어느 누구 못지 않게 훌륭한 선생이다.)

·He ran as quickly as possible. (he could)
(그는 가능한 한 빨리 달렸다.)

·She is as happy as can be.
(= She is as happy as anything.)
(그녀는 더할 나위없이 행복하다.)

(2) 우등(열등)비교

두 개 중에서 어느 한 쪽이 다른 쪽보다 우등(또는 열등)함을 나타내는 표현 방식

① more + 원급 + than ~ : ~ 보다 더 …하다.
동일한 사람(물)의 다른 성질을 비교 (음절수와 무관)
② less + 원급 + than~ : ~ 보다 덜 …하다.
= not so + 원급 + as~, rather… than ~
③ 비교급 ~ than any other + 단수 명사
비교급 ~ than all the other + 복수 명사
비교급 ~ than anyone(thing) else
부정어구 ~ 비교급 + than ~
〈비교급 → 최상급〉
④ the + 비교급 + of the two : 둘 중에서 더 ~한 쪽
⑤ the + 비교급 + S + V ~, the + 비교급 + S'+ V'~ : ~하면 할수록 더욱 …하다.
⑥ (all, so much) the + 비교급 + for(because of, on account of, owing to, because + 절, …): ~하기 때문에 오히려 더…
⑦ 비교급 + and + 비교급 : 점점 ~, 차츰 ~
⑧ no less ~ than … (= just as~as…): ~못지않게, 같을 정도로
not less ~ than … (= probably more ~ than): ~ 못지않게
no less than (= as much(many) as): ~만큼
not less than (= at least): 적어도
⑨ no more ~ than (= not ~ any more than …): ~아닌 것은 …아닌 것과 같다.
not more ~ than : ~만큼 …아니다.
no more than (= only): 단지
not more than (= at most): 기껏해야

She is more kind than (She is) generous ………………ⓐ

(그녀는 관대하기 보다는 친절하다.)

She is kinder than her sister (is kind)………………ⓑ

(그녀는 그녀의 누이보다 친절하다.)

[주의] 동일인(물)의 다른 성질을 비교할 때에는 낱말의 음절수와 관계없이 무조건 「more +원급 + than」의 형식으로 나타내고, 서로 다른 사람(물)의 다른 성질을 비교할 때에는 규칙(또는 불규칙) 변화를 적용하여 「비교급 + than」의 형식을 취한다.

She works more diligently than her sister (does).

(ex) It is colder today than (it was) yesterday.

His salary is lower than his wife's.

·This book is less interesting than that one.

(= This book is not as(or so) interesting as that one.)

(이 책은 저 책보다 덜 재미있다.)

·The higher we climbed, the colder the air became.

(높이 올라가면 갈수록 공기는 더욱 차가워져 갔다.)

·The younger the child is, the dearer it is to you.

(아이는 어릴수록 더 귀여운 것이다.)

·The more one has, the more one wants.

(사람은 소유하면 할수록 더 소유하기를 바란다.)

·Minae is the kindest girl is the class.

(= Minae is the kinder than any other girl is the class.)

(= Minae is the kinder than all the other girls in the class.)

(= Minae is the kinder than any one else in the class.)

(= No other girl is the class is kinder than Minae.)

(민애는 학급에서 가장 친절한 소녀이다.)

·I like her all the better for her kindness.

(= I like her so much the better because she is kind.)

(= I like her all the better because of her kindness.)

(나는 그녀가 친절하기 때문에 오히려 더 그녀를 좋아한다.)

[주의] 비교급 the better를 강조하기 위해 그 앞에 「all, so much, none」 등을 둘 때가 있다.

·She is none the wiser because she read many boods.

(많은 책을 읽었다고 해서 더 현명해지는 것이 아니다.)

(3) 최상급의 비교

세 개 이상의 사이에서 가장 정도가 높음을 나타내는 방식이다.

① the + 최상급 + of + 복수명사 (같은 종류)
the + 최상급 + in + 단수명사 (단체, 지역) 〉~ 중에서 가장 …

② one of (among) the + 최상급 + 복수명사 : 가장 ~한 중의 하나

③ the + 서수사 + 최상급 ~ : …번째로 ~한

④ the least + 원급 : 가장 ~이 아닌

⑤ the + 최상급 + 명사 + than 절

⑥ the most unlikely + 명사 + to + 동·원
the last + 명사 + to + 동·원 〉가장(결코) ~이 아닌

·Gold is the most valuable of all mentals.

(금은 모든 금속 중에서 가장 값비싼 것이다.)

·Mother is the earliest riser in my family.

(어머니께서 가족 중에서 가장 일찍 일어나신다.)

·Winston churchill was one of the greatest statesmen of the twentieth century.

(윈스턴 처칠은 20세기의 위대한 정치가들 중의 한 명이다.)

·She is the most beautiful girl that I have ever seen.

(그녀는 내가 이제껏 보아 온 소녀들 중에 가장 아름다운 소녀이다.)

·Chicago is the second largest city in the U.S.

(시카고는 미국에서 두 번째로 큰 도시이다.)

·She is the least beautiful of the three girl.

(그녀가 세 명의 소녀들 중에 가장 못생긴 소녀이다.)

·This is the least expensive method.

(이것은 돈이 가장 적게 드는 방법이다.)

·He is the least man to tell a lie.

(그는 결코 거짓말을 할 사람이 아니다.)

〈최상급 비교에서 주의해야 할 사항들〉

원칙적으로 형용사의 최상급에는 정관사 "the"를 붙이지만 부사의 최상급에는 붙이지 않는다. 그러나 최상급의 형용사라 하더라도 다음과 같은 경우에는 정관사 "the"를 붙이지 않는다.

□ 같은 사람(사물)에 있어서 성질과 상태의 비교, 다른 부분과의 비교, 시간에 있어서의 비교를 나타내는 경우

·This lake is deepest at this point.
(이 호수는 이 지점이 가장 깊다.)
·This lake is the deepest is Korea.
(이 호수가 한국에서 가장 깊다.)
·She is happiest when she is studying English.
(그녀는 영어 공부할 때 가장 행복해 한다.)
·She is the happiest of her friends.
(그녀는 그녀의 친구들 중에 가장 행복한 사람이다.)
·The typhoon will become most violent toward morning.
(그 태풍은 아침쯤에서 가장 난폭해질 것이다.)

□ 보어로 쓰여 단순히 뜻만을 강조하는 경우

·This article is cheapest.
(이 물건은 아주 싸다.)
·The soldier is (the) bravest of all. 〈가끔 the를 쓰는 경우도 있음〉
(그 군인이 가장 용감하다.)

□ 최상급 앞에 (대)명사의 소유격, any, no, that, another, 서수 등이 쓰이게 되는 경우

·You are my best friend.
(너는 나의 가장 친한 친구이다.)
·"A farewell to arms"is perhaps Hemingway's greatest novel.
("무기여 잘 있거라"라는 책은 아마도 헤밍웨이의 가장 유명한 소설일 것이다.)

□ 절대최상급: 비교의 대상을 확실히 나타내지 않고 막연히 정도가 높음을 표시하는 경우

·She was standing there with <u>a most</u> peculiar expression on her face.

(= very)

(매우 묘한 표정을 짓고서 그녀는 그곳에 서 있었다.)

□ "most"가 단독으로 「대개의 ~, 대부분의 ~」라는 뜻으로 쓰이는 경우.

·Most girls are interested in dresses.
(대부분의 소녀들은 옷에 관심을 가지고 있다.)

□ 부사의 최상급

·I like spring best.
(나는 봄을 가장 좋아한다.)
·He runs fastest of us.
(그는 우리들 중에서 가장 빨리 달린다.)
·He laughs best who laughs last.

(최후에 웃는 자가 가장 잘 웃는다.)

·I drives most carefully.

(나는 대단히 조심스럽게 운전을 한다.)

(4) 라틴어계의 비교급

「- or」의 형태인 라틴계의 비교급에는 "than" 대신에 전치사 "to"를 쓴다. 그러므로 그 뒤에 (동)명사가 온다는 점에 주의해야 한다.

① superior to : ~보다 월등한
inferior to : ~보다 열등한
② junior to : ~보다 손아래인
senior to : ~보다 손위인
③ interior to : ~보다 내부의
exterior to : ~보다 외부의
④ anterior to : ~보다 앞의
posterior to : ~보다 뒤의
⑤ major to : ~보다 큰
minor to : ~보다 작은
⑥ preferable to : ~보다 좋아하는
prefer to : ~보다 더 좋아하다

·He is five years senior to me.

(= He is five years my senior.)

(= He is my senior by five years.)

(= He is five years older than I.)

(= He is older than I by five years.)

(그는 나보다 5년 손위이다.)

C 기본 문형 익히기 Basic Sentence Drill

1. My old dog was big. → <u>My new dog is bigger</u>(형용사 비교급).

2. My old earrings were pretty.

→ ______________________________

3. His former secretary was careless.

→ His new ______________________________

4. The former president of Korea was powerful.

→ The new president of Korea is ______________________

5. Our old paster was competent in his ministry.

→ ______________________________

6. We had bad neighbors but we now have much ________ neighbors.

7. There are many apples in this box but in that box there are much ________ apples.

8. When you discover that you have a cancer for the treatment of disease, the sooner, ________.

9. My mother is as busy ever ________.

10. My husband is old and my mother is even ________.

11. Mary is ________ than any other girl in this class and it means she is ________ girl in the class.

12. In possessing the property, the more you have ________ you want.

13. The Apostle Paul is considered as the ______ _________ theologian in New Testament.(가장 영향력이 있는)

14. The virus of polluted air is as _________ as the sand on the seashore.

15. For Koreans English is not so easy as their native language to learn. German would be ______ _________ than English for them to learn.(더 어렵다)

D 응용 영작 Advanced Composition

Level 1

① 나는 *숲속의 새보다 *더 행복하다.

:

② 우리 엄마는 그 누구보다 더 지적(知的)이다.

:

Level 2

① *가능한 한 빨리 학교로 오십시오.

:

② 나는 내 누이동생보다 6년 더 위(연상)입니다.

:

Level 3

① 한국은 *동남아시아에서 가장 빠른 *교회 성장률을 가지고 있습니다.

:

② 과거의 소련과 미국은 가장 위험한 위기(고비)를 *겪었습니다.

:

▸ **Word Tips for composition**

* 숲속의 새: a bird in the woods
* 더 행복하다: ~ier than
* 가능한 한 빨리: as soon(early) as possible
* 동남아시아에서: In Southeast Asia
* 교회 성장률: the rate of church growth
* 겪었습니다: had gone through

E 응용 독해문 Applied Passages

Huntsville, TEXAS(AP)

Karla Faye Tucker, the pickax killer whose born-again Christianity sparked a worldwide debate over redemption and retribution on death row, was executed for hacking a man and woman to death during a 1983 breakin.

Ms. Tucker, 38, was declared dead by injection at 6:45 p.m. Tuesday.

She became the first woman executed in Texas since the Civil War.

"I'm going to be face to face with Jesus now," Ms. Tucker said in her final words.

"I love all of you very much I will see you all when you get there.

I'll wait for you."

The execution came less than an hour after the U.S. Supreme Court rejected an 11th-hour appeal and Gov. George W. Bush refused to grant a 30-day reprieve, saying her case had been thoroughly reviewed by appellate courts.

Worldwide publicity over Ms. Tucker's case, including pleas for mercy from Pope John Paul II and TV evangelist Pat Robertson, focused on her metamorphosis from a drug-crazed teen-age prostitute to a soft-spoken young woman who would be complicated with a life sentence.

F 관련 성경구절 Related Expression in the Bible

① Jeremiah 33:22(예레미야 33:22)

I'll make the descendants of David my servant and the Levites who minister before me as *countless as the stars of sky and as *measureless as the sand on the seashore.

(하늘의 만상은 셀 수 없으며 바다의 모래는 측량할 수 없나니 내가 그와 같이 내 종 다윗의 자손과 나를 섬기는 레위인을 번성케 하리라 하시니라.)

* countless: 셀 수 없는
* measureless: 측량할 수 없는

② Matthew 10:16(마태복음 10:16)

I am sending you out like sheep among wolves. Therefore be as *shrewd as snakes and as *innocent as doves.

(보라 내가 너희를 보냄이 양을 이리 가운데 보냄과 같도다. 그러므로 너희는 뱀

갈이 지혜롭고 비둘기같이 순결하라.)

* shrewd: 지혜로운, 빈틈없는, 영리한
* innocent: 순결한, 순수한

③ Psalms 19:10(시편 19:10)

They are more precious than gold, than much pure gold; they are sweeter than honey, than honey from comb.

(금 곧 많은 정금보다 더 사모할 것이며 꿀과 송이꿀보다 더 달도다.)

④ Genesis 41:39(창세기 41:39)

Since God has made all this known to you, there is *no one so *discerning and wise *as you.

(하나님이 이 모든 것을 네게 보이셨으니 너와 같이 명철하고 지혜 있는 자가 없도다.)

* not so ~as (no one ~ as): ~만큼 ~하지 못하다
* discerning: 명철한, 분별력 있는

⑤ Ephesians 3:8(에베소서 3:8)

Although I am less than *the least of all God's people, this grace was given me: to preach to the *Gentiles the *unsearchable riches of Christ.

(모든 성도 중에 지극히 작은 자보다 더 작은 나에게 이 은혜를 주신 것은 측량할 수 없는 그리스도의 풍성을 이방인에게 전하게 하시고)

* the least: 지극히 작은 자. little - lest -least (형용사 비교)
* Gentiles: 이방인들
* unsearchable: 측량할 수 없는, 헤아릴 수 없는

CHAPTER VII

가정(假定)법 문장 이용 말하기

Lesson 13

If I had not come and spoken to them, they would not be guilty of them.

가정법(Subjunctive Mood)의 종류와 용법 이용

A 성경 독해 NIV Reading

John 15:22-24

22 If I had not come and spoken to them, they would not be guilty
of sin. Now, however, they have no excuse for their sin.

23 He who hates me hates my Father as well.

24 If I had not done among them what no one else did, they would
not be guilty of sin. But now they have seen these miracles, and
yet they have hated both me and my Father.

한글성경 참조

요한 15:22-24

22내가 와서 그들에게 말하지 아니하였더라면 죄가 없었으려니와 지금은 그 죄를 핑계
할 수 없느니라

23나를 미워하는 자는 또 내 아버지를 미워하느니라

24내가 아무도 못한 일을 그들 중에서 하지 아니하였더라면 그들에게 죄가 없었으려니
와 지금은 그들이 나와 내 아버지를 보았고 또 미워하였도다

B 관련문법 Related Grammar Review

가정법(Subjunctive Mood)

1. 법(Mood; 法)이란 무엇인가?

어떤 사실이나 생각 또는 감정 따위를 나타낼 때 말하는 사람의 기분에 따라 그 표현이 달라질 수 있는데, 그러한 사람의 심적인 상태를 서술할 때 쓰이는 동사의 형태로 「직설법 동사·명령법 동사·가정법 동사」 등 세 가지가 있다. 이것을 법(法)이라고 한다.

직설법(Indicative Mood): 사실을 있는 그대로 서술하는 표현법.

·He is an honest man.

(그는 정직한 사람이다.)

명령법(Imperative Mood): 부탁이나 명령·요구·금지의 형식으로 자기의 의사를 상대방으로 하여금 실행하게 하려는 표현법.

·Be an honest man.

(정직한 사람이 되어라.)

가정법(Subjunctive Mood): 사실을 있는 그대로 서술하는 것이 아니라 상상적이고 소원적인 어투로 자기의 의사를 상대방한테 표현하는 방법.

·If he were an honest man, I marry him.

(만약 그가 정직한 사람이라면 나는 그와 결혼할 수 있을텐데-그러나 실제는 정직하지 못하기 때문에 결혼할 수 없다.)

2. 가정법(假定法)의 종류와 용법

가정법에는 가정법 현재(Subjunctive Present)·가정법 미래(Subjunctive Future)·가정법 과거(Subjunctive)·가정법 과거완료(Subjunctive Past Perfect)의 네 종류가 있는데, 이들의 명칭은 사용되고 있는 동사의 형태(시제)에 따라 분류시킨 것임을 주의해야 된다. 단, 가정법 미래는 그것이 나타내는 의미에 따라 명칭이 붙여졌다. 그러므로 가정법 미래를 제외한 가정법의 명칭은 그것이 나타내는 시제와 일치하지 않음을 주의해야 한다.

* 가정법의 종류

	종류	의미	조건절	주절
반대 사실	가정법 과거	현재 사실의 반대를 가정	If + S'+ 과거동사'+ ~ be 동사는"were"	would(의지), could(가능) should(무의지), might(추측) + 동·원
	가정법 과거 완료	과거 사실의 반대를 가정	If + S' + had + p·p + ~	would(의지), could(가능) should(무의지), might(추측) + have + p·p
불확실한 사실	가정법 현재	현재 또는 미래의 단순한 가정·의심	If + S' + 원형동사'+ ~ *직설법 현재동사도 씀	will, shall can, may + 동·원
	가정법 미래	미래에 대한 강한 의심	If + S' + should(무의지) + would(의지) + 동·원'	would·will(의지) should·shall(무의지) + 동·원
비현실		전혀 불가능한 미래 사실	If + S' + were to + 동·원'	would·should + 동·원

cf) "If"의 용법

① 조건·가정: 만약에 ~이라면

② 양보: 설령 ~일지라도(= though, although, while)

③ 명사절을 이끌어서 「~인지 어떤지(= whether)」로 해석

그러므로 조건절을 유도하는 "if"는 조건(가정)·양보의 두 가지 의미로 해석된다.

(1) 가정법 현재

: 현재 또는 미래에 대한 불확실한 가정(상상)과 의심을 표현할 때 쓴다.

> If + S'+ 원형동사(또는 직설법 현재동사) + ~,
> S +will, shall, can, may + 원형동사 + ~

[주의] 현재의 의지 또는 상대방의 의향을 나타낼 때는 if 절 속에 "will(would)"를 쓸 수도 있다.

·If you will sit down for a few moments, I'll tell him that you're here.

·If you would care to leave your name, I'll get in touch as soon as possible.

ⓐ If he is(be) honest, I will employ him. 〈현재〉

(만약에 그가 정직하다면 나는 그를 고용하겠다.)

ⓑ If it rains(rain) tomorrow, I will not go fishing. 〈미래〉

(만약에 내일 비가 온다면 나는 낚시하러 가지 않겠다.)

ⓒ If she is(be) old, I will employ her. 〈양보적인 해석〉

(= Though she is old, I will employ her.)

(설령 그녀가 늙었을지라도 나는 그녀를 고용하겠다.)

ⓐ에서 "If"는 "그가 정직한지 어떤지를" 모르고 있는 상태에서 단순히 가정(상상)을 해 본 것에 불과하다. 즉, 이면에는 「잘은 모르겠지만」이라는 50%의 가능성으로 말하고 있다고 볼 수 있다.

ⓑ에서도 마찬가지로 "If"는 "내일 비가 올지 안 올지"에 대해 모르고 있는 상태에서 단순히 불확실한 의심을 해 본 것에 지나지 않는다.

ⓒ에서는 "If"를 가정(조건)으로 해석하면 「만약에 그녀가 늙었다면 나는 그녀를 고용 하겠다」인데 어딘가 어색한 해석이 된다. 그러나 "If"를 양보로 해석하면 「설령 그녀가 늙었을지라도 나는 그녀를 고용 하겠다」라고 해야 앞뒤의 의미가 맞는다. 그러므로 "If"의 해석은 조건(가정) 또는 양보의 두 가지 의미가 있다.

(2) 가정법 미래

가정법 현재보다도 훨씬 불확실한 현재 또는 미래에 대한 가정을 나타낸다. 조건절 속의 동사는 두 가지가 이용되는데 미래에 어떤 동작이 일어날 수 있지만 그 가능성이 별로 없는 경우에는 「should」를 쓰고, 미래에 전혀 실현성이 없는 가정을 나타낼 때는 「were to」를 쓴다. 그래서 그 이면에는 "그럴 리는 없겠지만~"이라는 의미가 포함되어 있다고 볼 수 있다. 그러므로 이 가정법 미래는 어떤 일의 가능성이 극히 적어서 어느 정도 확신을 가지고 있는 상태에서 가정이라 할 수 있다.

	will, shall	
If + S'+ should(were) + 동·원'+ ~, S +	shall(should)	+ 동·원 + ~
	can(could)	
	may(might)	

* 특히, "주어의 강한 의지"를 나타낼 경우에는 조건절의 조동사를 「would (=wish to)」로 쓴다.

·If you would succeed, you would have to study hard.
(성공하려면 더욱 열심히 공부해야만 합니다.)
·If you should cause a traffic accident, your life would be ruined.
(〈그럴 리는 없겠지만〉 만일에라도 교통사고를 일으키면 당신의 인생은 끝장이 될 것이다.)
·If I should fail, I will(would) try again.
(만일에라도 실패한다면 나는 다시 시도하겠다.)
·If I were to be born again, I would be a teacher.
(만일에라도 내가 다시 태어난다면 선생님이 되겠다.)
·If(= though) the river were to flow back, I would not break the promise.

(설령 강물이 거꾸로 흐른다 할지라도 나는 그 약속을 깨지는 않겠다.)

(3) 가정법 과거

현재사실의 반대를 가정할 때 쓰이는 것으로 「만일 ~하면 …할텐데」라고 해석하는데 그 이면에는 「실제는 ~하지 않으므로 …할 수는 없다」라는 뜻을 가지고 있다. 특히 주의해야 할 사항은 사용된 동사의 시제가 과거형이라고 해서 나타내는 시제가 과거의 일이 아니라 현재의 일을 언급하고 있다는 것이다. 그러므로 이 가정법 과거는 명백한 기정사실을 정반대로 가정할 때 쓴다.

If + S'+ 과거동사(be동사는 항상 were to) + ~, S + would / should / could / might + 동·원

(= 직설법 : As + S'+ 현재동사의 부정 + ~, S + 현재조동사의 부정 + 동·원~.)

*그러나 가정법 과거가 부정문의 형태이면 그것의 직설법은 긍정문의 형태를 취하게 된다.

·If I had a job, I could pay back the money.
(= As I don't have a job, I can't pay back the money.)
(만일에 내가 직업이 있다면 그 돈을 갚을 수 있을 텐데.
- 즉, 지금 나는 직업이 없기 때문에 그 돈을 갚을 능력이 없다.)

·If she were good and diligent, I would employ her.
(= As she isn't good and diligent, I will not employ her.)
(만약에 그녀가 착하고 부지런하다면 나는 그녀를 고용할 텐데.
- 즉, 그녀가 착하지도 부지런하지도 않기에 그녀를 고용하지 않은 것이다.)

(4) 가정법 과거완료

과거사실의 반대를 가정할 때 쓰이는 것으로 「만일 ~했다면 …했을 텐데」라고 해석하는데, 그 이면에는 「실제는 과거에 ~하지 않았기 때문에 …할 수 없었다」라는 뜻을 가지고 있다. 특히, 주의해야 할 사항은 사용된 동사의 시제가 과거완료형이라고 해서 그 나타내는 시제가 과거 이전의 일이 아니라 과거의 사실 그 자체를 언급하고 있다는 사실이다.

If + S'+ had + p·p + ~, S + {would / should / could / might} + have + p·p

(= 직설법 : As + S'+ 과거동사의 부정 + ~, S + 과거형조동사의 부정 + 동·원~.)

·If she had helped me, I could have done it with ease.
(= As she didn't help me, I couldn't do it with ease.)
(만약 그녀가 나를 도와주었더라면 내가 그것을 쉽게 할 수 있었을 텐데.
- 그러나 그녀가 나를 도와주지 않았기에 나는 그것을 쉽게 할 수 없었다.)

C 기본 문형 익히기 Basic Sentence Drill

① What would you do if you had a Sabbatical year?

: I would travel around the world and research.

② What would you do if you won the lottery?

* probably quit my job을 써서

:

③ What would you do if you became the president of your country?

* change our society를 써서

:

④ If he is truthful, I __________ talk with him again.

⑤ If I __________ a child, I won't waste my time.

⑥ If I __________ a job, I could pay back the money.

⑦ I wish I __________ speak English well.

⑧ The child talks as __________ he __________ an adult.

⑨ __________ children make noises, __________ you be patient?

⑩ If it __________ be fine tomorrow, I __________ climb the mountain.

D 응용 영작 Advanced Composition

Level 1

① 만약 그녀가 너라면, 그녀는 그의 *제안을 받아들일 것이다.

:

② 만약 김 교수님이 이 반을 가르친다면, 그는 어떤 *시험도 치르게 하지 않을 것이다.

:

Level 2

① 만약 네가 *비밀을 지킨다면 아는 네게 선물을 줄 것이다.

:

② 내가 키가 좀더 컸더라면 나는 *미인대회에서 이겼을 것이다.

:

Level 3

① 내가 매일 아침 식사를 *거른다면 나는 *영양실조로 시달릴 것이다.

:

② 그가 늘 비타민 C를 복용했었다면 그는 암으로 죽지 않았을 텐데.

:

▸ Word Tips for composition

* 제안을 받아들이다: accept one's proposal
* 시험을 치루다: give a test
* 비밀을 지키다: keep the secret
* 미인대회: beauty contest
* (식사를) 거르다: skip
* 영양실조: malnutrition

E 응용 독해문 Applied Passages

But if we can gain that much insight, if we have become interested in the judgement of God, how shall we stand in that judgement?

How shall we become right with God; The most obvious answer is: "By obeying the law of God, by being what God wants us to be."

There is absolutely nothing wrong in theory about that answer; the only trouble is that for us it does not work.

If we had obeyed the law of God, if we were what God wants us to be, all would no doubt be well; we could approach the judgement seat of God and rely simply upon His judgement of the facts.

F 관련 성경 표현 Related Expression in the Bible

① Exodus 21:2(출애굽기 21:2) → 가정법 현재

If you buy a Hebrew servant, he *is to serve you for six years. But in the seventh year, he shall go free, without paying anything.

(네가 히브리종을 사면 그가 육 년 동안 섬길 것이요, 제칠년에는 값없이 나가 자유할 것이며)

* be to: ~할 것이다. ~할 예정이다.

② Job 5:8(욥기 5:8) → 가정법 과거

But if it were I, I would appeal to God; I would lay my cause before him.

(나 같으면 하나님께 구하고 내일을 하나님께 의탁하리라.)

③ II Kings 5:13(열왕기하 5:13) → 가정법 과거완료

My father, if the prophet had told you to do some great thing, would you not have done it?

(내 아버지여 선지자가 당신을 명하여 큰 일을 행하라 하였더면 행치 아니하였으리이까?)

④ Hosea 8:7(호세아 8:7) → 가정법 미래

It will produce no flour. *Were it to yield grain, foreigners would swallow it up.

(이삭은 열매를 맺히지 못할것이요 설혹 맺힐지라도 이방 사람이 삼키리라.)

* were it to grain~ ⇒ If it were to yield grain, foreigners would swallow it up.

⑤ Mattew 8:31(마태복음 8:31) → 가정법 현재

If you *drive us out, send us into the herd of pigs.

(만일 우리를 쫓아내실진대 돼지떼에 들여 보내소서.)

* drive out: 추방(축출)하다. 쫓아내다 = cast out, expel out, exclude, deport

Appendix

선교 실용영어

Appendix 선교 실용영어

*** 차재국, 『선교 영어회화 & 영어 기도법』 보강 부록편**

1 개인 종교에 대한 물음

A. Questions

1) What kind of religion do you have? (어떤 종류의 종교를 갖고 계십니까?)

2) What is your religion? (당신의 종교는 무엇입니까?)

3) Please tell me what your religion is. (당신의 종교가 무엇인지 말씀해 주십시오.)

4) May I ask you of your religion? (당신종교가 무엇인지 물어도 됩니까?)

5) Would/Could you please tell me what your religion is? (당시의 종교가 무엇인지 말씀해 주시겠습니까?)

6) Do you mind telling me something about your religion? (당신종교를 말씀해주셔도 괜찮으시겠습니까?)

B. Answers

m a Buddhist. (저는 불교도입니다.)

2) I am a Confucius. (저는 유교도입니다.)

3) I am a Muslim. (저는 회교도입니다.)

4) I am a Hindu. (저는 힌두교입니다.)

5) I am a Taoist. (저는 도교입니다.)

6) I am an Atheist. (저는 무신론자입니다.)

7) I am a freethinker. (저는 자유사상가입니다.)

8) I am a Unbeliever. (저는 불신자입니다.)

· Buddhism 불교
· Confucianism 유교
· Taoism 도교
· Christianity 기독교
· Pantheist 범신론자
· Atheist 무신론자
· Monotheist 유일신론자
· Theist 유신론자
· Deist 이신론자

2 기독교인인 경우

A. Questions

1) Are you a Christian? (당신은 크리스천입니까?)

2) Do you believe in God? (당신은 하나님을 믿습니까?)

3) Do you trust in God? (당신은 하나님을 믿습니까?)

4) Do you believe in Jesus Christ? (당신은 예수 그리스도를 믿습니까?)

5) Do you trust in Jesus Christ? (당신은 예수 그리스도를 믿습니까?)

6) Do you accept Jesus as your savio(u)r? (당신은 예수를 당신의 구세주로 받아들이십니까?)

7) Do you know who God is? (하나님이 누구인지 아십니까?)

8) Have you ever heard of Jesus Christ? (예수 그리스도를 들어보신 적이 있으십니까?)

9) You might be a Christian. (크리스천이신 것 같군요)

10) You must be a Christian. (크리스천이신 게 틀림없으시죠?)

11) You are a Christian, aren't you? (크리스천이시죠, 그렇죠?)

12) I suppose you are a Christian. (당신은 크리스천이것 같아요)

3 교회출석에 관한 질문

A. Questions

1) Which church do you attend? (어떤 교회에 출석하십니까?)

2) Which church do you belong to? (어느 교회에 소속해 계십니까?)

3) Which church are you from? (어느 교회 출신이십니까?)

4) Which church do you go to every Sunday? (매주일 어느 교회 나가십니까?)

5) What is the name of your church? (당신 교회 이름은 무엇입니까?)

6) What is the name of the church you attend/go to/belong to? (당신이 출석하시는 교회 이름은 무엇입니까?)

* 교단말하기 (church denomination)

· Presbyterian 장로교

· Methodist 감리교

· Baptist 침례교

· Full Gospel 순복음

· The Seventh-Day Adventist Church 안식교

· Holiness church 성결교

. Pentacostal Church 오순절 교회

4 What Denomination Does Your Church Belong to? (교단말하기)

1) What denomination does your church belong to? (당신의 교회는 어느 교파에 속해 있습니까?)
My church belongs to the Presbyterian denomination. (저희 교회는 장로교파에 속해 있습니다.)

2) What denomination do you belong to? (당신은 어느 교파에 속해 있습니까?)
I belong to the Presbyterian Church. (저는 장로교에 속해 있습니다.)

3) What denomination do you come from? (어느 교파 출신입니까?)
I come from the Baptist Church. (저는 침례교 출신입니다.)

4) What denomination are you from? (어느 교파 출신입니까?)
I'm from the Presbyterian Church. (저는 장로교회 출신입니다.)
*H*is denomination is a conservative one. (그의 교단은 보수 교단입니다.)
The doctrine of their denomination is liberal. (그들 교단의 교리는 자유주의적입니다.)
Their doctrine is heretical. (그들의 교리는 이단적입니다.)

*** 필수용어**

·the Methodist Church 감리교
·the Evangelical Church 복음주의
·the Full Gospel Church 순복음
·the Salvation Army Church 구세군
·the Lutheran Church 루터교
·the Reformed Church 개혁주의
·the Independence Church 독립 교회
·heretical 이단적인
·the Roman Catholic Church 천주교
·the Moonism, 통일교
The Unification Church
·the Jehovah's Witness 여호와의 증인
·the Mormonism 몰몬교
·Sabbath (The Church of Sabbath) 안식교
·The Seventh Day Adventist Church
·Syncretism 혼합주의
·Pluralism 다원주의
·the Baptist Church 침례교
·the Anglican Church 성공회
·the Holiness Church 성결교
·the Pentecost Church 오순절
·the Holy Spirit Church 성령주의
·the Orthodox Church 정교회
·heresy 이단

〈예배행정〉

5 Who Is Senior Pastor Of Your Church?

Who is senior pastor of your church? (당신 교회의 당회장 (시무) 목사님은)
The senior paster of our church is (the) Rev. Bill Kim.
(우리 교회의 시무 목사님은 빌 킴 목사님이십니다.)

*필수용어

1) 당회 The Church committee

2) 당회장The Chairman of Church committee(Senior Paster)

3) 부목사Associate Pastor

4) 전도사Evangelist Youth Pastor(美)

5) 교육전도사Assistant Pastor

6) 목사 Pastor, Minister, Reverend, Priest, Clergy

7) 장로 Elder

8) 권사 Senior Deaconess

9) 집사 Deacon/ Deaconess

10) 안수집사 Ordained Deacons

11) 서리집사 Temporary Deacons

*Church Administration (교회행정)

1) 총회 General Assembly

2) 노회 Presbytery Meeting

6 What Is the Membership Of Your Church?

1) What is the membership of your church? (귀하 교인의 교인 수는 몇 명입니까?)

About ten-thousand membership. (약 만 명가량 됩니다.)

2) How many members are there in your church? (귀하 교회의 교인 수는 몇 명입니까?)

There are some five hundred members in my church. (우리 교회의 교인 수는 약 500명입니다.)

3) How many members does your church have/hold? (귀하 교회의 교인 수는 몇 명입니까?)

We have around seven-hundred members in our church. (우리 교회 교인 수는 약 7백 명입니다.)

4) What is the seating capacity of your church? (당신의 교인 몇 명을 수용할 수 있습니까?)

My Church has a seating capacity of 5,000. (우리 교회에는 5천 명을 수용할 수 있는 좌석이 있습니다.)

5) How many people can your church accommodate? (당신의 교회는 몇 명을 수용할 수 있습니까?)

My church can accommodate 30,000 people. (우리 교회는 3만 명을 수용할 수 있습니다.)

***중요 어휘 연구**

·membership; (n) 회원 자격, 회원 수.

·congregation: 회중, 교인들.

·capacity; (n) 용적, 용량, 수용 능력.

·seating capacity; 수용 좌석 수.

·accommodation; (n) (교통수단에서의 승객을 위한) 좌석, 숙박 시설.

·accommodate; (v) ~을 수용하다, 수용 능력이 있다.

7 What Are You In Charge Of In Your Church?

1) What are you in charge of in your church? (교회에서 무슨 직분을 맡으셨나요?)

I am in charge of the Youth Group. (저는 청년회를 맡고 있습니다.)

*Sunday School 주일 학교
*High school Group 고등부
*College Group 대학부
*Church choir 성가대
*Youth Group 청년부
*Church choir director 성가대 지휘자
*Church orchestra 교회 관현악단
*Church choir accompasist(pianist) 성가대 반주자

2) What kind of position do you hold in your church? (교회에서 무슨 직책을 맡고 있습니까?)

I am a senior pastor. (저는 당회장 목사입니다.)

*preacher 강도사
*junior pastor(evangelist) 전도사
*student pastor 교육전도사
*elder (presbyter) 장로
*senior deacon(ess) 권사
*ordained deacon 안수집사
*deacon (deaconess) 서리집사

8 Please Let Me Hear Your Personal Testimony:

1) Please let me hear your personal testimony. (간증을 좀 들려주십시오.)

2) Could you please tell me your personal testimony? (간증을 좀 들려주실 수 있겠습니까?)

3) Would you tell me your personal testimony? (간증을 좀 들려주실 수 있겠습니까?)

4) Do you mind telling me your personal testimony? (간증을 좀 들려주시지 않으시겠습니까?)

5) Do you have any testimony to share with us? (우리에게 들려주실 간증이 있으신지요?)

6) Do you have any motivation for your converting into Christianity? (기독교로 개종하신 어떤 동기라도 있습니까?)

7) Would you tell me the motivation for your becoming a Christian? (기독교인이 되신 어떤 동기라도 있습니까?)

8) What made you a Christian? (어떻게 기독교인이 되셨습니까?)

***중요 어휘연구**

·testimony; (n) 증언, 증명, 신앙 선언.

·convert; (vt) ~을 전환시키다, 변환하다
개종시키다; (vi) 전환하다, 개종하다.

·motivation; (n) 동기

·share sth with sb; ~(무생물)을 ~(생물)과 나누어 갖다.

9 We Welcome You to our Church.

1) Is it your first visit to our church? (저희 교회에 처음 오셨습니까?)

Yes, I've never been here before. (네, 전에 한 번도 이곳에 온 적이 없습니다.)

Yes, this is my first visit here. (네, 이곳은 처음입니다.)

Yes, I'm totally stranger here in this church. (네, 이 교회에 완전히 처음입니다.)

2) We welcome you to our church. (저희 교회에 오심을 환영합니다.)

We welcome you to our church with warm Christian love. (저희 교회에 오심을 따뜻한 성도의 사랑으로 환영합니다.)

3) You are very welcome to our church. (저희 교회에 오심을 대단히 환영합니다.)

4) Welcome to our church. (저희 교회에 오심을 환영합니다.)

5) We are giving you our warm and hearty welcome. (귀하에게 따스하고 진심어린 환영을 보냅니다.)

6) Shall we give our warm welcome hands to Mr. &Mrs. Kim. (우리 다 함께 김 씨 부부에게 따스한 환영의 박수를 보낼까요?)

7) Let's give our hands to our sister Miss Lee who is a new comer today. (오늘 처음 나오신 이 양에게 박수를 보냅시다.)

8) Let's clap our hands to our brother James who has determined to accept Christ as his Saviour. (그리스도를 구주로 영접하시기로 작정하신 제임스 형제에게 갈채를 보냅시다.)

10 Were You Moved By The Pastor's sermon?

1) Were you moved by our pastor's sermon?

=Were you impressed by the pastor's message? (목사님의 설교에 은혜를 받으셨습니까?)

Yes, very much. (네, 무척요.)

Yes, I was moved by our pastor's sermon. (네, 목사님의 설교에 은혜를 받았습니다.)

2) What do you think of today's preaching?

=How do you like today's message? (오늘 설교를 어떻게 생각하십니까?)

I think it was just wonderful. (아주 훌륭하였습니다.)

It was really moving message. (정말 은혜스러운 말씀이었습니다.)

It was very impressive. (아주 은혜스러웠습니다.)

I like it very much. (매우 좋았습니다.)

It moved my heart. (은혜스러웠습니다.)

It was poignant. (심령을 찌르는 말씀이었습니다.)

***중요 어휘연구**

·be moved by; ~에 마음이 움직이다.

·be impressed by; ~에 감명 받다.

·sermon; 설교

·preach; 설교하다. preaching; 설교

·message; 전달문, 통지, (기독교에서는 흔히) 설교.

·poignant; 가슴에 사무치는, 마음을 찌르는.

=moving

11 Do You Attend every Official Worship?

1) Do you attend every official worship? (모든 공 예배에 출석하십니까?)

Yes, I do. (네, 그렇습니다.)

Yes, I relatively do. (네, 비교적 그렇습니다.)

Yes, I try to do so. (네, 그렇게 하려고 노력하는 편입니다.)

No, I attend only Sunday service. (아니오, 전 단지 주일예배만 출석합니다.)

No, I attend only Sunday morning service.

2) Do you attend early morning prayer meeting?

=Do you participate in early morning prayer meeting?

(새벽기도회에 출석하십니까?)

Yes, I do. (네, 그렇습니다.)

Yes, at least more than five days in a week. (네, 적어도 일주일에 5일 이상은 참석합니다.)

Seldom. (거의 참석하지 못합니다.)

No, I can't get up early in the morning. (아니오, 전 일찍 일어날 수 없습니다.)

No, I'm afraid I'm a late sleeper. (아니오, 전 새벽잠이 많습니다.)

3) Do you attend Wednesday prayer service? (수요 기도회에 참석하십니까?)

Yes, I usually do so. (네, 일반적으로 그렇게 합니다.)

4) Do you attend Friday overnight prayer meeting?

=Do you participate in Friday overnight prayer meeting?

(금요 철야기도회에 참석하십니까?)

Yes, I do. (네, 그렇습니다.)

Yes, I often do. (네, 자주 참석하는 편입니다.)

No, I'm afraid I'm too busy every Friday. (아니오, 매주 금요일마다 너무 바빠서요.)

No, I'm too lazy to do so. (아니오, 너무 게을러서요.)

No, never. (아니오, 아직 한 번도 못했습니다.)

5) How often do you attend early morning prayer meeting? (새벽기도회에 얼마나 자주 참석하십니까?)

I attend early morning prayer meetings at least for three says a week. (저는 새벽 기도회에 일주일에 적어도 3일은 참석하는 편입니다.)

I attend for seven days per week. (저는 일주일에 7일 꼬박 참석합니다.)

I seldom go to the early morning prayer meeting. (저는 거의 참석하지 못합니다.)

I cannot get up at five in the morning. (저는 5시에 일어나질 못합니다.)

Five o'clock is too early for me to get up. (5시는 일어나기엔 너무 이른 시간인 것 같아요.)

I've never ever got up early in the morning. (저는 도저히 아침 일찍 일어나지 못합니다.)

I'm a sleeper. So I usually get up at eight or nine. (저는 잠꾸러기입니다. 그래서 8시나 9시에 일어납니다.)

The Oder of the Worship Service at Kosin University Church

(고신대학교 교회 주일 오전 예배 순서)

Rev. & prof. C. Kee Hwang, Th.D. : Senior Pastor

(황창기 목사, 신학박사: 담임목사)

·Prelude (전주)

·Greetings (인사)

·Announcement (광고)

·God Calls Us (하나님께서 우리를 부르십니다)

·Invocation (기원)

·Psalm of Praise (찬양)

·God Cleanses Us (하나님께서 우리를 깨끗이 하십니다)

·Confession of Sins (죄의 고백)

·Declaration of Forgiveness (사죄의 은총 확인)

·Response to God's Declaration (하나님의 사죄에 화답)

·Doxology (송영)

·Psalm of the Week (금주의 시편)

·Hymn of praise (찬송)

·Prayer of praise (기도)

·God Instruct Us (하나님께서 우리를 가르치십니다)

·Scripture (성경)

·Sermon (설교)

·Response to God's Words (하나님의 말씀에 화답)

·The Creed (사도신경)

·Anthem (특송)

·Offering (연보)

·Pastoral Prayer and Lord's Prayer (목회기도 및 주기도)

·God Feeds Us (하나님께서 우리를 먹이십니다)

·Response to God's Gift (하나님의 선물에 화답)

·Prayer of Thanksgiving (감사기도)

·Closing Hymn (폐회찬송)

·God commissions Us (하나님께서 우리를 일터로 보내십니다)

·Charge (부탁)

·Benediction (축도)

·Response to God's Charge (하나님의 부탁에 화답)

·Threefold Amen (삼중아멘)

·Welcoming new Winners (새 신자 환영)

1) Before our worship service, let's exchange greetings with each other. 예배 전에 서로 인사를 교환하십시다.

2) Rev. Hwang will preside at this worship. 황 목사님께서 본 예배의 사회를 보시겠습니다.

3) God is calling us. We should respond to His calling with pleasure. 하나님께서 우리를 부르십니다. 기꺼이 그의 부르심에 화답합시다.

4) Let's praise the Lord. 하나님을 찬양합시다.

5) Rev. Hwang will pray for us. Let us pray together. 황 목사님께서 기도 인도하시겠습니다. 다 함께 기도합시다.

6) Now Rev. Hwang will preach a sermon. 이제 황 목사님께서 설교하시겠습니다.

7) We welcome you to our church with warm Christian greetings. 저희 교회에 오신 것을 성도의 사랑으로 뜨겁게 환영합니다.

8) We love you with the love of Jesus Christ. 예수 그리스도의 사랑으로 사랑합니다.

13 The Kinds Of Prayer(기도의 종류)

-The Lord's Prayer (주기도문)
-The Apostles' Creed (사도신경)
-The Benediction (4 examples) (축도; 4종류)
-A General Thanksgiving (일반적인 감사기도)
-Grace (식사기도)

1) The Lord's Prayer(주기도문)

Our Father, ①which (who) ②art (are) in heaven,
hallowed be Thy name, Thy Kingdom come,
Thy will be done, on earth as it is in heaven.
Give us this day our daily bread;
and forgive us our trespasses,
as we forgive them that trespass against us;
and lead us not into temptation, but deliver us from evil.
For thine is the kingdom, the power, and the glory, for ever and ever.
Amen.

하늘에 계신 우리 아버지여
이름이 거룩히 여김을 받으시오며
나라가 임하시오며
뜻이 하늘에서 이루어진 것 같이 땅에서도 이루어지리다
오늘 우리에게 일용할 양식을 주시옵고

우리가 우리에게 죄지은 자를 사하여 준 것 같이
우리 죄를 사하여 주시옵고
우리를 시험에 들게 하지 마시고 다만 악에서 구하시옵소서
나라와 권세와 영광이 아버지께 영원히 있사옵나이다
아멘

① which = 고어에서 who
② art = be의 주어가 2인칭 단수일 때

2) The Apostles' Creed(사도신경)

I believe in God the Father Almighty, Maker of heaven and earth:
And in Jesus Christ His only son our Lord, who was Conceived by the Holy Ghost, born of the Virgin Mary, suffered under Pontius Pilate,
He descended into hell; The third day He rose again from the dead;
He ascended into heaven, and sitteth on the right hand of God the Father
Almighty; From thence he shall come to judge the quick and the dead.
I believe in the Holy Ghost; The Holy Christian (catholic) church,
the Communion of Saints; The forgiveness of sins; The resurrection of the body, and the life everlasting. Amen.

나는 전능하신 아버지 하나님, 천지의 창조주를 믿습니다.
나는 그의 유일하신 아들, 우리 주 예수그리스도를 믿습니다.
그는 성령으로 잉태되어 동정녀 마리아에게서 나시고,
본디오 빌라도에게 고난을 받아 십자가에 못 박혀 죽으시고,
장사된 지 사흘 만에 죽은 자 가운데서 다시 살아나셨으며,

하늘에 오르시어 전능하신 아버지 하나님 우편에 앉아 계시다가,
거기로부터 살아 있는 자와 죽은 자를 심판하러 오십니다.
나는 성령을 믿으며, 거룩한 공교회와 성도의 교제와
죄를 용서받는 것과 몸의 부활과 영생을 믿습니다. 아멘.

3) The Benedictions(축도)

The grace of our Lord Jesus Christ, and the love of God,
and the Communion of the Holy Spirit, be with you all.
Amen.

주 예수 그리스도의 은혜와 하나님의 사랑과 성령의 교통하심이 너희 무리와 함께 있을 지어다. (고후 13:13)

The Lord bless you and keep you. The Lord make His face to shine upon you and be gracious unto you. The Lord lift up His countenance upon you, and give you peace. Amen.

여호와는 네게 복을 주시고 너를 지키시기를 원하며, 여호와는 그 얼굴로 네게 비취사 은혜 베푸시기를 원하며, 여호와는 그 얼굴을 네게로 향하여 드사 평강주시기를 원하노라. (민 6;24~25)

The peace of God which passeth all understanding, keep your hearts and minds in the knowledge and love of God, and of His Son, Jesus Christ, our Lord; and the Holy Spirit be, upon you and remain with you always. Amen.

헤아릴 수 없는 하나님의 평강이 너희의 심령과 마음을 지키셔서 하나님과 그의 아들 예수 그리스도 우리 주를 알고 사랑하게 하시옵시며, 성령이 너희 위에 항상 있을지어다.

Now the God of peace, that brought again from the dead our Lord Jesus, that great shepherd of the sheep, through the blood of the everlasting covenant, make you perferct in every good work to do His will, working in you that which is well-pleasing in His sight, through Jesus Christ, to whom be glory for ever and ever. Amen.

양의 큰 목자이신 우리 주 예수를 영원한 언약의 피로 죽은 자 가운데서 이끌어 내어 평강의 하나님이 모든 선한 일에 너희를 온전케 하사 자기 뜻을 행하게 하시고 그 앞에 즐거운 것을 예수 그리스도로 말미암아 우리 속에 이루시기를 원하노라. 영광이 그에게 세세 무궁토록 있을지어다.

4) A general thanksgiving(일반적인 감사기도)

Almighty God. Father of all mercies, we Thine unworthy servants do give Thee most humble and hearty thanks for all Thy goodness and loving kindness to us, and to all men. We bless Thee for our creation, preservation, and all the blessings of this life; but above all, for Thine inestimable love in the redemption of the world by our Lord Jesus Christ for the means of grace, and for the hope of glory. And, we beseech Thee, give us that due sense of all Thy mercies, that our heart may be unfeignedly thankful, and that we shew forth Thy praise, not only with lips, but in our lives; by giving up ourselves to Thy service, and by walking before Thee in holiness and righteousness all our days;

through Jesus Christ our Lord, to whom with Thee and the Holy Ghost, be all honor and glory, world without end. Amen.

전능하신 하나님, 자비가 풍성하신 아버지, 당신의 천한 종들이 저희를 향하신 당신의 모든 선하시며 친절한 사랑에 겸허하고도 진실 어린 감사를 드립니다. 저희를 창조하시고, 보호하시고, 이렇게 삶의 축복을 주심을 충심으로 감사드립니다. 그러나 무엇보다도, 우리 주 옛 그리스도로 말미암아 세상을 구원하신 측량할 수 없는 사랑과, 은혜의 수단과 영광의 소망을 갖게 하심을 감사드립니다. 또한 간구하옵는 것은 주님의 모든 인자하심을 분별할 수 있게 하여 주옵시고, 저의 심령이 진심으로 감사하게 하옵시며 입술로만이 아니라 삶 속에서 주님을 찬양하게 하옵소서. 우리자신들을 바쳐 주님을 위해 봉사하게 하시고, 우리가 사는 날 동안 주님 앞에서 거룩함과 의로 걸어가게 하소서. 성부 그리고 성령과 함께, 모든 존귀와 영광을 영원히 돌릴 예수 그리스도 우리 주님의 이름으로 기도합니다.

14 Prayers by Topics(주제별 기도문)

1) Let us Pray(기도를 위한 기도)

Lord, teach us how to pray aright,
With reverence and with fear;
Though dust and ashes in thy sight,
We may, we must, draw near.

God of all grace, we come to thee
With broken contrite hearts;
Give, what thine eye delights to see,
Truth in the inward parts;

Faith in the only sacrifice
That can for sin atone;
To cast our hopes, to fix our eyes,
On Christ, on Christ alone.

Give these, and then thy will be done;
Thus, strengthened with all might,
We, through thy Spirit and thy Son,
Shall pray and pray aright.
We pray in the name of Jesus, thy only Son.

주여, 우리에게 올바른 기도법을 가르쳐 주옵소서.
존경과 경외하는 마음으로 기도하는 법을 말입니다;
주님 보시기에는 비록 티끌이나 재 같을 지라도,
우리들을 주님 가까이 이끄소서.

모든 은혜를 베푸시는 하나님, 하나님께 나아갑니다.
통회 자복하는 마음으로;
하나님 보시기에 즐겨 하시는 것,
마음속에 진리를 주시옵소서.

유일한 희생양을 믿는 믿음으로
죄를 속할 수 있나이다;
우리의 소망들을 그리스도에게,
우리의 안목들을 그리스도에게만 고정시키게 하소서.

이러한 것들을 주옵시고, 하나님의 뜻을 이루어 주소서;
그리하여, 전능으로 강하게 하옵소서.
하나님의 영과 아들을 통하여,
우리로 하여금 기도하게 하소서, 합당한 기도를.
독생자 예수님의 이름으로 기도 드립니다.

Heavenly Father, we come to you in the greatness of your love and lift up our hearts in prayer and praise.
We thank you that the way to your presence is always open through Jesus Christ and that you invite us to draw near in full assurance of faith.

Help us to pray simply and sincerely, unselfishly and gratefully, remembering the needs of others as well as our own, and giving thanks always for all things in the name of Christ our Lord.

하늘에 계신 아버지, 크신 주의 사랑으로 당신께 나아갑니다.
기도와 찬양으로 우리의 마음을 올려 드립니다.
예수 그리스도를 통하여 당신의 존전으로 나아가는 길이 항상 열려 있음을 감사하오며,
확신에 찬 믿음으로 우리를 당신 가까이로 초대하시니 감사합니다.
우리로 단순히, 성실히, 이기심을 버리고, 감사하는 마음으로 기도하게 하시고,
우리의 필요와 다른 사람들의 필요를 기억하게 하시고, 항상 범사에 감사하게 하소서.
예수님의 이름으로 기도 드립니다.

We thank you, Lord Christ ,for the promise of your presence to the two or three who gather in your name.
Help us to remember that you are with us now as we meet together to pray.
Make us of one heart and mind, that we may agree in what we ask; and as we ask in your name, so may we pray in accordance with your will, and glorify our Father in heaven.

주 그리스도여, 주님의 이름으로 모이는 두세 사람에게 함께 하시겠다고 약속하신 것을 감사합니다.
우리가 함께 만나 기도하는 이 시간 주님께서 우리와 함께 하심을 기억하게 하소서.
우리의 마음과 정신이 하나 되게 하셔서, 우리가 같은 것을 구하게 하시고, 우리가

주님의 이름으로 구하는 것 같이 하나님의 뜻에 따라 구하게 하시고, 하늘에 계신 우리 아버지를 영화롭게 하게 하소서.

2) Giving Thanks (감사의 기도)

O God of love, make us more thankful
for all the boundless mercies of our daily life.
Forgive us that we are so often ungrateful,
complaining and discontented,
taking for granted your greatest gifts:
the blessings of health,
the comforts of home and family life,
the joys of friendship, the wonders of your creation.
Teach us day by day to number our blessings
and to receive each one as from our Father's hand;
and fill our lives with gratitude,
our lips with praise;
for the sake of Jesus Christ our Lord.

오 사랑의 하나님, 날마다 저희들의 살에 무한하신 자비를 베푸신 하나님께 더욱 감사를 드립니다.
감사치 못하고, 불평하며, 불만족하며, 하나님의 크신 은사들;
건강의 축복들,
편안한 가정생활,
친구와의 즐거운 우정 생활,
경이로운 하나님의 창조의 솜씨들을

당연하게 여기는 저희들을 용서하소서;
날마다 하나님의 축복들을 헤아려 보게 하시고, 이 축복들이 하나님의 손길로부터 온 것임을 알게 하시고, 우리의 삶 속에서 감사가 충만케 하시고, 우리의 입술로 찬양케 하소서;
우리 주 예수 그리스도의 이름으로 기도합니다.

3) Christian Marriage (기독교적 결혼)

God our Father, who made men and women to live together in families: we pray that marriage may be held in honour; that husbands and wives may live faithfully together, according to their vows; and that the members of every family may grow in mutual love and understanding, in courtesy and kindness, so that they may bear one another's burdens and so fulfil the law of Christ; for his name's sake.

남자와 여자를 만드시고 함께 가족으로 살아가게 하신 하나님 우리 아버지,
결혼이 명예롭게 이루어지게 하시고, 온 가족이 서로의 사랑과 이해와 예의와 친절 안에서 자라가게 하셔서, 서로의 짐을 지게 하시고, 그리스도의 법을 지키게 하소서.
예수님의 이름으로 기도합니다.

4) The birth of a child(출생)

Heavenly Father, how good you are!
How wonderful are your works!
We praise you for all your gifts and especially for your gift to us of this dear child.
We take him to our hearts and welcome him to our home as a token of your love; and gratefully we give him back to you, to love and serve you all his days, in the name of Jesus our Lord.

하늘에 계신 아버지, 당신이 얼마나 선하신지요!
당신의 솜씨가 얼마나 놀라우신지요!
당신이 주신 모든 선물들을 인하여 찬양 드리오며, 특별히 이 귀여운 아기를 선물로 주신 것을 찬양합니다.
이 아이를 우리의 마음에 받아들이며, 당신의 사랑의 증표로 우리 가정에 영접 합니다; 감사하는 마음으로 이 아이를 당신께 되돌려 드리오니, 이 아이의 일생 동안 당신을 사랑하며 섬기게 하옵소서. 우리 주 예수 그리스도의 이름으로 기도 드립니다.

5) The blessing of a new home(새 가정을 위한 축복)

Lord, bless this house and al who live in it.
Hallow it with your presence and your peace.
Let it be a place where prayer is made,
Where love abounds,
Where your name is honoured;
and may your fatherly hand be over us day by day,

in our going out and coming in,
now and for evermore.

주여, 이 집을 축복하시고, 그 속에 거하는 모든 이들을 축복하소서.
주님의 임재와 평안으로 이 집을 거룩하게 하소서.
기도가 이루어지는 곳이 되게 하시고,
사랑이 넘치는 곳이 되게 하시고,
주님의 이름으로 존귀히 여겨지는 곳이 되게 하시고,
우리가 나가고 들어갈 때,
지금과 영원토록
날마다 아버지의 손길이
우리 위에 넘치게 하소서.

6) Daily work(매일의 직업을 위한 기도)

Lord Jesus Christ, we thank you that you have taught us,
by word and example, the dignity and sanctity of all honest work.
Help us in our daily duties to follow in your steps:
to be faithful in whatever we undertake,
to give always of our best,
and in all things to act as your servants;
to the glory of God the Father.

주 예수 그리스도여, 말씀과 본으로 모든 정직한 일의 존엄성과 고결함을 우리에게 가르쳐 주시니 감사합니다.
우리들의 매일 맡은 일속에서 당신의 발자취를 따르게 하옵소서;

우리가 맡은 것은 무엇이든지 성실히 행하게 하옵시며,
우리의 최선을 다하게 하옵시며,
모든 일에 당신의 종으로 행하게 하옵소서;
하나님 아버지의 영광을 위해서.

7) For one in hospital(환자를 위한 기도)

Our loving Father, from whose mighty hands
all life and healing come,
have now within your own intensive care
this suffering one dear to us.
Give sleep tonight, give peace of heart,
and freedom from anxious fear,
that healing may be quietly at work.
And since there is oneness in the face of sickness,
let this your servant have an open heart
to lift the hope of others who are there:
to show that love of yours
which never lets us go, nor ever fails,
wherever we may be, whatever pain we suffer.

사랑하는 아버지, 하나님의 능하신 손에서
모든 생명과 나음이 나옵니다.
하오니 우리에게 소중한 이분의 고통을
하나님께서 친히 강하게 보살펴 주옵소서.
오늘 밤 수면을 주시고, 마음의 평안을 주시고,

근심과 공포에서 벗어나게 하셔서
고요한 중에 나음을 입게 하옵소서.
병마에 꿋꿋이 맞서서,
당신의 종이 마음을 열게 하시고,
함께 있는 다른 사람들에게 소망을 나타내게 하시며,
당신의 사랑을 보여주게 하셔서,
우리가 어디에 있든지, 어떤 고통을 당하든지,
실족하거나 실패하지 않게 하소서.

8) The dying(임종을 위한 기도)

We pray, O Lord for your servant-whose life is drawing near its end. Give him your peace in his heart.
May he know the Saviour's presence with him and rest his faith wholly is Him; that through your redeeming love he may enter into your etermal joy and join the heavenly host who live and praise you for evermore.

오 주님, 지금 생명의 종말이 가까운 당신의 종을 위항 기도드립니다.
그의 마음속에 당신의 평안을 주옵소서.
그에게 구세주의 함께하심을 알게 하시고,
전적으로 그분께만 믿음을 두게 하소서; 당신의 구속적 사랑을 통하여
당신의 영원한 기쁨에 들어가게 하시며
영생하며 당신을 찬양하는 천국의 주인의 자리에 동참하게 하소서.

9) The mentally ill(정신적 고통을 당한 분을 위한 기도)

Heavenly Father, we remember to our comfort that you have in your special care all broken, outworn and imperfect minds.
Give to those who live with them and minister to them the understanding and loving Spirit Christ.
Enlighten those who are tempted to laugh at such illness or regard it with shame; and to all who are thus separated in this life by barriers of mind, grant the peace and consolation of your Holy Spirit; through Jesus Christ our Lord.

하늘에 계신 아버지여, 당신께서는 상하고, 지치고, 불완전한 모든 마음들을 특별히 돌보아 주심을 우리가 기억하므로 위로가 됩니다.
그들과 함께 살며, 그들을 보살피는 자들에게 그리스도의 이해의 영과 사랑의 영을 주옵소서.
그러한 질병을 비웃거나 창피스럽게 여기고 싶은 유혹을 느끼는 자들을 깨우쳐 주소서;
그리고 정신적 장벽으로 이 세상 삶에서 소외된 모든 자들에게 성경의 평강과 위로를 허락하여 주옵소서; 우리 주 옛 그리스도의 이름으로 기도 드립니다.

10) Our neighbours(이웃을 위한 기도)

Heavenly Father, we thank you for our neighbours and for the people around us with whom we share our daily lives.
We prat for those who are old and lonely; those isolated because of ill-health; and those who find it difficult to make friends.
Show us what we can do to help, and teach us to be good neighbours; for Jesus' sake,

하늘에 계신 아버지, 우리에게 매일의 삶을 함께 나눌 수 있는 이웃과 주위의 사람들을 주심을 감사합니다.
연로하시고 의로운 사람들과 건강으로 격리된 사람들과 친구들 사귀기 어려운 사람들을 위하여 기도드립니다.
그들을 도울 수 있는 방법을 가르쳐 주시고, 그들에게 좋은 이웃이 되는 길을 가르쳐 주소서;
예수님의 이름으로 기도 드립니다.

11) A prayer for peace(평화를 위한 기도)

Give peace in our time, O Lord;
peace and reconciliation among the nations;
peace and unity within the churches;
peace and harmony in our communities and our homes;
peace and love in all our hearts;
for the sake of Jesus Christ, our Saviour.

오 주여, 우리 시대에 평화를 주시옵소서;
국가과 국가 사이에 평화와 화해를;
교회 내에 평화와 단결을;
우리의 지역사회와 가정에 평화와 일치를;
우리 모두의 가슴에 평화와 사랑을 주옵소서.
우리 구주 예수 그리스도의 이름으로 기도합니다.

12) The local church(지역 교회를 위한 기도)

Thank you, Lord. for local church;
for those who have worshipped in it over the years
and for those who serve it today.
Grant that all who enter its doors
may be enabled to renew their relationship with you
and may find your peace, your strength, your grace,
and above all your presence.
Help us as a congregation to be outward looking,
so that what we find within our fellowship
we may share with those outside,
for the benefit of all and for your greater glory,
in Jesus Christ our Lord.

주여, 우리 교회를 주심을 감사드립니다.
오랜 햇수 동안 그곳에서 예배를 드리는 사람들과
오늘 교회를 섬기는 자들을 인하여 감사드립니다.
교회 문을 드나드는 모든 자들을 축복하셔서

그들이 당신과 새로운 관계를 맺을 수 있게 하시고,
당신이 주시는 평화와 능력과 은혜와
무엇보다도 다인의 임재를 맛보게 하소서.
우리가 회중으로서 우리의 안목을 밖으로 돌리게 하셔서,
우리들의 교제를 교회 밖에 있는 자들과 나누게 하시며,
모든 사람에게 유익을 끼치며, 당신께 더 큰 영광을 돌리게 하옵소서.
우리 주 예수 그리스도의 이름으로 기도 드립니다.

13) Before worship in church(예배 전 준비기도)

Heavenly Father, draw near to us as we draw near to you now in this hour of worship.
Open our hearts to receive all that you have to give to us, and graciously accept all that we have to offer you, in the name of Jesus Christ our Lord.

하늘에 계신 아버지, 저희가 당신께 나아가는 이 예배 시간에 저희 가까이 오시옵소서.
당신이 우리에게 주시고자 하는 모든 것을 받을 수 있도록,
그리고 우리가 당신께 바쳐야 할 모든 것을 기꺼이 바칠 수 있도록 저희의 마음을 열어 주옵소서.
우리 주 예수 그리스도의 이름으로 기도 드립니다.

14) Holy Communion(성찬식 기도)

Come to us, Lord Jesus, in your risen power
when we receive the bread of life and the cup of salvation.
Cleanse our hearts from sin, that they may be worthy of so great a guest; and keep us abiding in your love, for your great name's sake.

주 예수여, 저희가 생명의 떡과 구원의 잔을 받을 때에,
당신의 부활의 능력으로 저희들에게 찾아오소서,
저희의 마음을 죄에서 깨끗이 씻어 주셔서,
성찬에 참여하는데 합당한 마음이 되게 하시며,
저희를 당신의 사랑 안에 계속 거하게 하소서.
주님의 위대한 이름으로 기도 드립니다.

15) The baptism of a child(유아 세례 기도)

Lord Jesus Christ, we thank you for your love for little children.
When you were here on earth, you welcomed those who were brought to you, took them into your arms and blessed them.
May your blessing be upon our dear child whom we bring to you in baptism, to be received into the family of your Church.
Grant that he may grow up to be a faithful member of that family, and may learn to love and serve you all his days; for your name's sake.

주 예수 그리스도여, 어린 아기를 사랑하여 주시니 감사드립니다.
당신께서 이 땅에 계시는 동안, 당신은 당신에게 나아오는 아기를 환영하시고,

팔에 안으시사 복을 주셨습니다.
세례를 통하여 우리가 주님께로 데려와, 교회의 한 가족이 되기를 원하는 이 사랑스러운 아이에게 당신의 축복이 임하옵소서.
이 아이가 이 가정의 신실한 믿음의 구성원이 되게 하시고 항상 주 예수를 사랑하고 섬기는 것을 배우게 하옵소서.
주 예수님의 이름으로 기도하옵니다.

성경 66권 발음 익히기

1. 구약성서(Old Testament)

Genesis 창세기
Exodus 출애굽기
Leviticus 레위기
Numbers 민수기
Deuteronomy 신명기
Joshua 여호수아
Judges 사사기
Ruth 룻기
First Samuel 사무엘상
Second Samuel 사무엘하
First Kings 열왕기상
Second Kings 열왕기하
First Chronicles 역대상
Second Chronicles 역대하
Ezra 에스라
Nehemiah 느헤미야
Esther 에스더
Job 욥기
Psalms 시편
Proverbs 잠언
Ecclesiastes 전도서
Song of Songs 아가
Isaiah 이사야
Jeremiah 예레미야
Lamentations 예레미야애가
Ezekiel 에스겔
Daniel 다니엘
Hosea 호세아
Joel 요엘
Amos 아모스
Obadiah 오바댜
Jonah 요나
Micah 미가
Nahum 나훔
Habakkuk 하바국
Zephaniah 스바냐
Haggai 학개
Zechariah 스가랴
Malachi 말라기

2. 신약성서(New Testament)

Matthew 마태복음

Mark 마가복음

Luke 누가복음

John 요한복음

The Acts 사도행전

Romans 로마서

First Corinthians 고린도전서

Second Corinthians 고린도후서

Galatians 갈라디아서

Ephesians 에베소서

Philippians 빌립보서

Colossians 골로새서

First Thessalonians 데살로니가전서

Second Thessalonians 데살로니가후서

First Timothy 디모데전서

Second Timothy 디모데후서

Titus 디도서

Philemon 빌레몬서

Hebrews 히브리서

James 야고보서

First Peter 베드로전서

Second Peter 베드로후서

First John 요한일서

Second John 요한이서

Third John 요한삼서

Jude 유다서

The Revelation 요한계시록

선교영어회화 English For Mission

1판 1쇄 인쇄_2014년 02월 02일
1판 1쇄 발행_2014년 02월 10일

지은이_한귀란
펴낸이_홍정표

펴낸곳_글로벌콘텐츠
등록_제 25100-2008-24호

공급처_(주)글로벌콘텐츠출판그룹
이사_양정섭 디자인_김미미 편집_노경민 김현열 김다솜 기획·마케팅_이용기 경영지원_안선영
주소_서울특별시 강동구 천중로 196 정일빌딩 401호 전화_02-488-3280 팩스_02-488-3281
홈페이지_www.gcbook.co.kr

값 12,800원
ISBN 979-11-85650-14-2 03740